LIVING ON THE SEABED

A Memoir of Love, Life and Survival

Lindsay Nicholson

Vermilion
LONDON

1 3 5 7 9 10 8 4 2

First published in the United Kingdom in 2005 by Vermilion

This edition published in 2006 by Vermilion,
an imprint of Ebury Publishing
Random House UK Ltd.
Random House
20 Vauxhall Bridge Road
London SW1V 2SA

Randon House Australia (Pty) Limited
20 Alfred Street, Milsons Point, Sydney,
New South Wales 2061, Australia

Random House New Zealand Limited
18 Poland Road, Glenfield, Auckland 10, New Zealand

Random House (Pty) Limited
Isle of Houghton, Corner of Boundary Road & Carse O'Gowrie
Houghton 2198, South Africa

Random House Publishers India Private Limited
301 World Trade Tower, Hotel Intercontinental Grand Complex,
Barakhamba Lane, New Delhi 110 001, India

Random House UK Limited Reg. No. 954009
www.randomhouse.co.uk
Papers used by Vermilion are natural, recyclable products
made from wood grown in sustainable forests.

A CIP catalogue record is available
for this book from the British Library.

ISBN: 0091906822
ISBN: 9780091906825 (from Jan 2007)

Printed and bound in Great Britain by
Bookmarque Ltd, Croydon, Surrey

INTRODUCTION

I'm at a dinner party and this woman across the table from me wants to know if I have a husband, a partner? 'No,' I mumble, 'I'm a single parent.' 'Poor you, what happened, did he run off?' 'No,' I mumble again. 'He's just not around.'

The conversation becomes general. The woman is sounding off about men who abandon their children. 'How old was your daughter when he left you?' she calls across the table. And something snaps inside me. 'He died,' I correct her. 'He died of leukaemia when my eldest child was three and I was pregnant with our second.'

She blanches but then recovers. 'You only have one child,' she retorts – as if I am lying. 'Yes,' I say driving the knife hard into the heart of the dinner party babble. 'Ellie died, too. Six years later. From leukaemia as well.' In the utter silence that descends on the dinner table I regret my words. Not because I spoke the truth but because I spoke at all.

It's a wonder I'm ever invited anywhere really. In a world where even very intelligent people think that if they take vitamins they'll live to be 100, owning up to the dreadful truth that some people do die before their time is the adult equivalent of saying there is no Santa Claus, Tooth Fairy or Easter Bunny.

To lie, to deny John and Ellie's existence, is unthinkable. Yet I have to go out and live the life that I am left with, so usually I'm evasive when people ask about my family. But then someone will press too hard and the grief comes spilling out, engulfing everyone around me.

∞

Time is not the universal healer. As it passes you do adjust to life without the person you love but I don't think you ever really get over the death of a partner or a child. You just get better at putting on a public face. The pain is always there.

As a child I was obsessed with, and appalled by, the story of *The Little Mermaid*. In the Hans Christian Andersen version – not the Disney one – when the Little Mermaid gets her wish and is allowed to live on dry land, every step she takes is like walking on knives. I agonised for her. How could she do it? How could you live with unbearable, unending agonising pain? Surely the human spirit could not take it – or mine couldn't anyway. And then I found out that it could. I don't suppose an hour of the day goes by when I don't think of John and Ellie but like the Little Mermaid this is what it takes for me to breathe air.

I remember the day after my husband John died, waking up in the morning and being utterly enraged that the sun was still shining. It seemed almost obscene that it could be a lovely day when my world had been destroyed.

Of course, people expect the bereaved to hide themselves away – ideally reclining on a *chaise longue* dabbing gently at the eyes with a lace-trimmed handkerchief, only to emerge sane and recovered after a decent interval.

But grieving takes literally years and years. Not in the movies, of course, where it takes around three months – six weeks in a very bad movie. But in real life you've got to allow at least four long years – often a lot more. And the reason they speed it up in the movies is that it's boring. Even if you cry for four hours a day – which is a hell of a lot of crying – that still leaves 20 to be got through. Plus most people have to earn a living. I know I did. It was balm to my soul, distracting me from the horror that was my life.

And I went to dinner parties – and probably ruined them. Some people never spoke to me again. I reckon that, post-bereavement, you can count on losing up to a third of your Christmas card list, which is hurtful – especially as it can be the people you thought would always be there. But it balances out because into your life come new friends and you see sides to old friends that you never knew existed.

∞

In August 2002 I met with Ian Katz, features editor of *The Guardian*, for lunch at The Clerkenwell Dining Room. Ostensibly we were there to talk about the consumer testing that the Good Housekeeping Institute was carrying out for *The Guardian* – which was the best washing machine, toaster, vacuum cleaner; that sort of thing. But the conversation turned around to my personal history. Ian has the incorrigible curiosity of a child. But what was it like, he kept asking me. How did you feel? How did you cope?

I didn't take offence. I couldn't. His interest was genuine and unlike most people he didn't shy away from talking about the Greek tragedy that had been my life. In the end he told me I must write a piece for *The Guardian* because he'd never seen anything written about the long-term effects of bereavement. You see lots, he said, written in the short-term, the aftermath, but nothing about what it's like day in, day out, year in, year out.

So I agreed. And in September I sent him a very professional (I'm a writer and editor after all) 1,500-word piece about bereavement and its impact on society and individuals. I included plenty of quotes and statistics to back up my arguments. To my absolute horror, he rang me a week later and said it wasn't at all what he was look-ing for. It's a very professional piece, he agreed, but it's written by someone looking in from the outside. It's not how you spoke that day in the restaurant.

I was very shocked. No one had rejected my copy in years. But eventually I calmed down and started to try to write what we had spoken of in the restaurant. I couldn't. I was completely blocked. What I really felt was too awful, too horrible to commit to print. A month went by: I still couldn't do it. Eventually one afternoon, when I couldn't stand it hanging over me any longer, I knocked back a couple of glasses of wine, sat down in front of the computer and just typed.

As I typed I started to cry. And I cried and typed for three solid hours. At the end I was snotty-nosed and puffy-eyed – and had written 3,500 words. None of it seemed to make any sense to me. There was no logic, no structure and certainly no happy ending. But I just didn't care any more. I didn't care what people thought of me. I didn't care that I'd owned up to some pretty rotten emotions, to overeating, chain smoking, drinking too much and having really bad sex with inappropriate men.

I was just so relieved to have got rid of the poison that had been clogging up my mind for years. All I cared about was that I'd got it out, that I'd stopped pretending that grief is pretty or decent or sensible or civilised. It's horrible, painful, jagged and dangerous. It makes you turn on people who care about you and it makes you wonder what on earth there is to go on living for when the people you love are dead. And although it changes and can, I fervently believe, become manageable, it never goes away.

I was exhausted with the effort of writing and I thought

it was probably unpublishable, but that was Ian's problem so I pressed Send on the computer and emailed it to him.

∞

He did run it. Unaltered and in its entirety, on 2 December 2002. It was a Monday and I arrived at work to find myself deluged with phone calls and emails and messages from people who'd read it. Friends, obviously, but also total strangers. The next day the letters arrived. Most of them started the same way: '*I thought I was going mad. I didn't know anyone else felt that way . . .*'

In February 2003 the *Mail on Sunday*'s *You* magazine reprinted the article and even more letters arrived. A typical one read: 'Two years ago my father died and now my marriage is breaking up. I thought I was just unlucky until I read your article and realised the two things might be connected. I showed it to my husband and we're talking now . . .'

Many of the letters started with apologies because the writer's experience was not as severe as mine – *just* the death of an aged parent or *just* a miscarriage, as if there were a hierarchy of grief. But there isn't. The finality of death is always horrible, always terrible and somehow has to be got through.

I am no better qualified than any other bereaved person to tell anyone else how to cope but writing that one newspaper article was cathartic for me and – from the letters I received – appeared to help some other people, too. So I decided to have a go at putting my thoughts down properly. I have always been a copious note-taker and diary-keeper so, however unlikely or unreasonable the feelings described appear to be, they are actually what I felt, thought and wrote at the time.

∞

However, I am not a medical expert and this book is not intended to give medical guidance. I have written about the conditions my husband and child suffered as best I can and according to my understanding of what was happening at the time. I have included only those details necessary to explore the feelings and emotions I was experiencing. The treatments they underwent have almost certainly been improved or superceded. But this is not intended to be a book about leukaemia. It's about grief. In particular about the four rules of grieving that I have learned over the years:

The first rule, obviously, is that it takes far, far longer than you think. If your marriage runs into trouble or your child has difficulties at school some two, three, or even more years after a bereavement – don't think the two aren't connected. They probably are.

The second rule is that the worst bit is not the death – although it might feel at the time as if it is. The worst bit actually comes months later when all the fuss has died down and your friends who were so helpful in the beginning have gone back to their own lives again. If you are reading this book soon after someone you love has died then that's absolutely the last thing you want to hear. But you need to know it because you need to plan ahead. And so do the people supporting you. All those people who write in the immediate aftermath saying 'anything, anything I can do' need to know that what matters most is still to be in touch in six months' time.

The third rule is that there will be a fight. This I can guarantee. You might think that you're not the argumentative kind. That falling out with people is hardly the way to honour someone's memory. But the fact is it will happen. Often at the funeral but certainly within the first year. You can't stop it happening just by being prepared, but you can prevent it from escalating out of control into a long-running feud.

The fourth rule is that anniversaries are hell. Always. Accept it and work around them.

It sounds grim and it is. For someone who has not experienced the loss of someone close to them it may sound unnecessarily depressing but my experience – and the experience of everyone else I have spoken to – is that if you know what you're in for then it's a lot less frightening than not knowing, and thinking that you are losing your mind into the bargain. I like to use the analogy of the natural childbirth movement in the Seventies. At that point, childbirth had gone from being a natural process, supervised largely by women working from their own experience, to a medical process kept separate from everyday life and shrouded in mystery. Of course, there were advantages to this in that some mothers and babies who might otherwise have died were undoubtedly saved. But there was a downside in that women who were giving birth for the first time found it even more painful and frightening than it need be, simply because they had no idea of what was normal and what wasn't. The natural childbirth pioneers never claimed that it wouldn't hurt but they did believe that if you knew what was coming you could work *with* the pain rather than fight it.

Death has also become medicalised. Again, for the very good reason that so many people can now be saved who otherwise would not be. But for those left behind this has led to a disenfranchisement which can make the mourning process harder even than it need be. Which is hard enough.

∞

As a young woman I didn't know what to expect of grief, and I fought and fought and fought it every inch of the way. This book is born out of that pain in the hope that my experiences might help someone else. There is a phrase I have had cause to use over and over again. It describes the period when you are absolutely at the lowest ebb. When the full horror of the death has sunk in and you can see no reason for joy or pleasure ever to exist in your life again. I call it crawling around on the seabed of despair. It is as if you are one of those dark creatures that lives on the ocean floor and has never felt the sun on its back. You can't go upwards to the light because you can't remember ever knowing the light. The only comfort is that you can't go any lower because there is nowhere else to go. All you can do is crawl around on the ocean floor with thousands of fathoms of water between you and the world where other people live. I spent several years on the seabed of despair. It would have helped me to know that someone else out there had gone through this experience and survived to see the light again. When I was down there, this is the book I would have liked to read.

Chapter One

∞

THOSE WERE
GOLDEN DAYS

I packed a small bag with her bloodstained pyjamas, the book she'd been reading, the teddy bear she called Apricot. Despite the fact that it was June and the weather was sunny, I felt cold so I put an old riding jacket over my business suit. Then we went to Paddington and caught the train to Plymouth. It seemed somehow fitting to be making this journey again – the one that had begun two decades before, back in the golden days.

∞

I had arrived at Plymouth Station for the first time in August 1978, with all my possessions packed in the three suitcases I'd been given for my twenty-first birthday, my father's old typewriter balanced on top. Could I walk to my new digs? Could I afford the fare for a taxi? Not really but I had no idea where I was going and the cases were heavy, so I took a cab anyway.

I had booked into a lodging house run by a woman called Dilys. She was a cut above the other landladies in the area as she took in arty types – actors appearing in the summer shows at the theatre on the Hoe and journalists training on the newspapers owned by the Mirror Group in the West Country. I was one of the latter. A real-live journalist. No longer a student, a whole world of new opportunities was about to open up for me.

One of the features of staying at Dilys's was that all her lodgers had to watch the TV soaps on permanent look-out for her 'boys and girls' who occasionally had walk-on parts. But that Sunday night there were no soaps to watch, so after a lonely supper I went to bed early ready for the next day, the first day of my new life.

In those days the Mirror owned a regional group called West of England Newspapers, to use as a base for training journalists. It was a royal road to a job on one of their nationals and places on the course were hard to come by. It was hugely prestigious and the year I applied there were 650 graduate applicants for six jobs. But it was a long way from Fleet Street.

The offices were sited on an industrial estate outside Plymouth and it was from here that the regional *Sunday Independent* and the weekly *Plymouth Times* were published. A Portakabin parked in the car park formed the makeshift classroom where our trainer, Cedric Pulford, set about telling the 12 of us – six graduates and six local school leavers – what was expected of journalists. Or actually he set about telling 11 of us, as one was inexplicably missing. First Cedric asked us if we all had cars. A car, he said, was vital for a reporter. Someone pointed out that we could hardly afford cars on the £16 a week we were being paid. I couldn't drive anyway so sank low in my seat and stared out of the window. I'd failed at the first hurdle. Maybe I wasn't cut out to be a journalist?

Someone was walking across the car park. I could only see the hair. It was the most unusual colour, not really red, more gold. A flash of gold. The owner of the hair came into the Portakabin apologising for being late, but he'd been out on a story – investigating the theft of supermarket trolleys in the suburb of Plymstock. His name was John Merritt and he was the missing twelfth trainee. Unlike the rest of us dutifully arriving on the first day as if we were still at school, he'd shown up at the start of summer, convinced the editor of the *Plymouth Times* to take him on and had actually covered stories and had his name in the paper already. My heart did a double flip. I fell in love with him at first sight. But then so, I'm sure, did everyone else in the room.

At the end of the first week, John asked me to accompany him to work on the news programme for the local hospital radio. So he was a broadcaster as well as a published journalist . . . I thought there was no end to his talents. And the following Friday he asked me out to dinner at the most expensive restaurant in Plymouth. I was duly impressed, as he'd hoped I would be. He ordered sole, I did likewise, and was appalled to discover it was served on the bone complete with head and dead fishy eyes. I suspect John was, too, but we both struggled to eat it.

After that, he didn't ask me out again. We were just together. There were no questions, no doubts, no anxieties. We were inseparable. He was 21. I had just turned 22. We had embarked on the careers of our dreams and each found the love of our life. I can picture us now in my mind's eye: both of us tall and slender, me with dark brown eyes and long, conker-coloured hair; John taller still, six foot at least, still with gangly boyish limbs and his astonishing red-gold hair and piercing blue eyes. We must have appeared truly blessed, a golden couple. There was no indication that John carried a deadly genetic trait that would rob him of his life as a young man and then kill his daughter, too. No one who knew us then would have doubted that we had anything other than a glorious future ahead of us. I didn't doubt it myself. Of course, I knew we would face difficulties together but everything in my life had taught me that if you worked hard enough and loved well enough then good things would surely happen.

It was a philosophy that worked in the past for my family.

∞

My father Anthony was born in 1929. His father Tom worked at the railway depot in Stratford, East London, and the family lived in a council house nearby. Emma, my paternal grandmother, worked as a cleaner but instilled in her children – my father and his younger sister Josephine – her belief that the only way out of the East End slums was through education. She sent Tony and Josephine, later known as Josie, or Jo, to local Catholic schools but her ambitions for them of a good education and qualifications were dashed by the Second World War. Both children were evacuated with their schools until Emma – unable to live without them – brought them back to the East End, saying: 'If we're going to be bombed we'll be bombed together.' And they were. They were forced out of their original house in Crowndale Road and had to move around the corner to Chandos Road, London E15.

Tony's schooling was badly interrupted although he was naturally bright and managed to matriculate at the age of 15. Further education was out of the question, so after National Service he dabbled in various jobs and wrote a play, *Vanguard*, based on his father's life on the railways. It was put on at the Theatre Workshop, Stratford East, by the director Joan Littlewood in a series of plays by local talent, and starred Harry H. Corbett who went on to play the younger Steptoe in the early sitcom *Steptoe and Son*. Tony was temporarily lionised as an 'angry young man' and as one of the so-called 'young meteors' of the early Fifties.

His parents couldn't support him, however, and he was unable to make a living as a writer, so he went into journalism as the next best thing, becoming acting editor of a tiny weekly paper, the *Laindon Recorder* in Essex. There he played host to a group of Young Conservatives who wanted to see around a newspaper office and was immediately attracted to their 19-year-old organiser, Sheila Pigram. She had jet black hair, green eyes and an 18-inch waist, but was an unlikely Young Conservative, growing up as she had in a bungalow built by her father a mile down an unmade road. It has since been subsumed by Basildon New Town but then Laindon was an unprepossessing country village popular with families who were moving out of the East End and the Dockland areas in search of fresh air and green fields.

Sheila's family had done just that and her father Albert, a maintenance enginer at Battersea Power Station, had built the family house himself although he never really finished it. One of my earliest memories is of a cement mixer parked in the front garden. Sheila, his second child, was bright, tough and ambitious but, as with Tony, an academic education was out of the question so she left school at 16 and trained as a hairdresser. She landed a job in a West End salon, where she went on the train every day, in clothes she'd sewn herself, smart copies of Christian Dior's New Look.

Her diaries at the time record a giddy teenage social life with theatre outings, tennis parties and campaigning for Bernard Braine, the local Conservative MP. But within a year of meeting Tony Nicholson they were married and had moved to Ipswich where he had got a job on the *East Anglian Daily Times*. I was born in 1956, a year after their marriage, when Sheila was 21 and Tony was 27.

Miles away from their families and unable to afford a car, or even the bus fare back to Essex, they pursued their dreams together. Believing there was little hope of supporting the family they wanted through journalism or writing, they agreed that Tony should read for the Bar. A fairly breathtaking decision for a young couple with a baby and no back-up – but made possible by the fact that they discovered he could study for his exams through a correspondence course and didn't need a college law degree.

To save money, they returned to London when I was 18 months old, moving in with Tom and Emma. Tony supported us in between his studies by working long shifts for the Extel News Agency. The house in Chandos Road was what you might expect of a council house in the Fifties. The tiny back yard was concreted over and still had the remains of the bomb shelter where the family had slept every night during the Blitz. There was no bathroom and no inside toilet. I didn't mind a bit. I loved the constant attention from four adults and the baths taken in the scullery with water heated in the old copper, from where – screened by washing drying on the clothes airer – I could chat to the rest of the family gathered in the kitchen.

My grandfather Tom came from a horse-racing family and his own father had been quite a well-known jockey so he liked to think he knew the horses. He would go to the betting shop on a Saturday – or, if he was feeling flush, to a race meeting. On Sunday lunchtime he'd take his winnings to the pub – or drown his sorrows there – tottering gently home at closing time to fall asleep for the afternoon on my bed. This was fine by me as when he woke up there'd be a plate of winkles for his tea and I would sit on his lap fishing them out for him with a pin, while he told me stories of horses that he called the 'gee-gees' and of the steam engines he'd worked on.

But my mother hated every day of living with her in-laws. She had brought with her a chic little black poodle that fought constantly with my grandmother's fat lazy cocker spaniel – just one of many ways in which she considered living in the East End vastly inferior to the bungalow in Laindon which, although it was never properly finished off, was at least in the countryside and owned by her family, not rented from the council. One of my earliest memories is of watching from the front room as she returned from a shopping trip wearing the smart clothes saved from her single days, black hair waved, nails and lips painted scarlet and head held high as she skipped briskly across the cobble stones, her mind fixed on the better future that she was sure was around the corner for her family. I doubt she was even 25 at the time.

To achieve this bright future no effort was too great, no expectation too high. Reading and education were paramount. Table manners were drilled into me from the moment I could grasp a knife and fork in my fat little paws. If I protested I would be told that I could never go to smart restaurants when I grew up if I didn't know how to eat properly. Baby words were banned, as was any trace of an East End or Estuary accent, which might hold me back in the glittering life that was planned for me. When I was three my mother took me on the underground from Stratford to the Royal Opera House, Covent Garden, to see a matinée of the ballet *Swan Lake*. I loved it and remember drinking real orange juice with bits in – the first time I'd ever tasted it – in the Crush Bar, then dancing every step of it right through for Emma and Tom when we got back to Chandos Road. The love of ballet has stayed with me my whole life and, more than 40 years later at a gala evening, I met Anya Linden, who by then was Lady Sainsbury, the ballerina who'd danced Odette/Odile that afternoon in 1959. I was too shy to tell her that in a trunk at home I still had the programme I'd saved from that day out.

I was five before my father finally qualified as a barrister and by that time had two baby brothers, Jeremy and Hugh, born just 16 months apart. Yet somehow Sheila and Tony had scraped together the deposit for a modest three-bedroomed house in the commuter town of Ingatestone, Essex. To subsidise his paltry earnings as a newly qualified barrister my father worked three nights a week as a night lawyer for the *Daily* and *Sunday Express*.

After finishing a day in court or in Chambers he would walk around to the black glass art deco building that was Beaverbrook House in Fleet Street, and work until one or two in the morning reading all the stories in the paper for possible libels or contempt of court. This was in its heyday when the *Express* sold millions of copies a day, and he was proud of the fact that he libel-read throughout the Profumo scandal without receiving a single writ.

Needless to say, his children saw very little of him. To me he became a distant and rather scary figure. I couldn't understand why he had to work so much because even despite the long hours there was little cash to spare. Our house was tiny with no room for a separate study so, on the nights when he was at home, he would prop a piece of chipboard across the arms of his favourite wing armchair as a make-shift desk and work through the evening, oblivious to the noise and chaos of family life going on around him. If we were lucky, though, he would break off at bedtime and make up stories for the three of us featuring characters called Dougal Dinwiddy, Septimus Peckinpah and Penelope Pecksniff (who was me, of course). They all lived on the Isle of Skye, which is where we believed the Nicholson name originated.

I was seven before we got a TV, telephone or a fridge. Central heating came even later. We had a car but for a while were unable to tax or insure it so it was jacked up on bricks while we travelled by bus. But to me the greatest hardship was that my mother made my school uniform. As stylish as ever, she interpreted the rules liberally and used whatever length of material she could pick up cheaply in the market. I loathed everything about home-made clothes, starting with standing on the kitchen table while she pinned the fabric to fit me, occasionally pricking my skin as she worked. I was once castigated during assembly in front of the whole school for wearing a mini-dress because according to the head teacher Sister Thecla: 'We don't like mini-dresses at this school.'

My Holy Communion dress was another of my mother's creations. I had wanted to wear white ruched netting like all the other little girls at my school but she'd produced from a length of white satin what was known at the time as a Twist Dress. The nuns termed it 'sinful'. The official photograph to commemorate my First Holy Communion shows me scowling and hunched with a school cardigan covering up the offending garment. I resolved like Scarlett O'Hara that when I grew up I would never wear home-made again.

More than anything else I wanted to fit in. But my parents had dedicated their lives to escaping their roots, not fitting in. When the money worries began to ease we acquired a huge Ford Zephyr, packed a tent on the roof rack and went camping across Europe for our summer holidays. My mother had got the idea for that from a magazine. All her ideas seemed to come from magazines. Despite having to have home-made clothes, home-cut hair and very, very plain home-cooked food (shop-bought cakes seeming to us children the height of luxury), my mother's one indulgence was glossy magazines and my father would buy them for her at Liverpool Street Station if he had time to kill waiting for a train. She especially liked *Nova*, and *Vogue* and *Good Housekeeping*. I would read and re-read them after she'd finished with them, saving them until they became dog-eared. Only then would I cut out the pictures to stick in scrap books and create magazines of my own.

I was always reading and writing stories, often late into the night to the exasperation of my grandmothers when they came to stay. My maternal grandmother Rose tried to defeat me by removing the light bulb from my bedroom altogether but there was a streetlamp outside and I read by that. When I wasn't reading I was dreaming of living in London in a flat with other girls, wearing fashionable clothes and working on a magazine.

I passed the 11+ with ease and won a direct grant place at the Ursuline Convent in Brentwood; and I was thrilled that the strict regulations meant my uniform had to be bought from a shop. It was, however, bought big enough to last me until the sixth form but like the other girls I quickly got the hang of rolling my brown pleated skirt up at the waist so that just an inch showed below my brown, blue and gold striped blazer.

In our family we never regarded ourselves as poor – we were always thinking of the next move on our upward trajectory. When I was 12 we were able to move to a bigger, four-bedroomed house down the road in Hutton. But not long after, I was awoken in the night by howls like a dog in pain. There were doctors, an ambulance, and my father was taken away to hospital. He was 39 and had testicular cancer – now often curable but in the late Sixties the prognosis was poor.

Self-employed with a non-working wife and three children, plus a huge mortgage, he had no choice but to work through his illness. I remember him sitting up in the hospital bed after his operation, writing up cases on foolscap legal pads. After he was discharged he had radio-therapy, often fitting it in around court appearances and then vomiting copiously on the way home. The serious-ness of his illness was never discussed with us children but we did know we were properly poor now.

My mother needed to go back to work and as soon as Hugh, the youngest, started school, she enrolled on a teacher training course at Brentwood College of Educa-tion. This made little or no difference to our means. That autumn was especially wet and I was furious when she told me that I had to wait until her termly grant cheque came through before I could have an umbrella to keep me dry on the way to and from school. I remember protesting bitterly that we'd all have been a lot better off if she had just gone back to being a hairdresser. She snapped that if she was going to leave her children to go out to work it was going to be for a good job – a response I disagreed with vehemently at the time but that clearly was to have an influence on me in later life.

We sold the new house and moved into a draughty old vicarage that was being sold off by the Commissioners of the Church of England as it needed so much work doing to it. It was in the village of Southminster, some 50 miles from London and over an hour by train to my school. Although it cost far less than our executive home in the commuter belt it was a beautiful and gracious Georgian house built for Dr John Scott who had been Nelson's chaplain at the battle of Trafalgar and later retired to Essex. In the space of 10 years my family had moved from a council dwelling with outside toilet in the East End to an historic country house with four reception rooms downstairs and a graceful oval staircase that curved up to seven bedrooms, and lots of nooks and hiding places besides. Best of all there was over an acre of garden for us kids to run wild in and it meant we could have more dogs, cats, chickens, at one time a falcon, and eventually a pretty grey pony for me called Trophy, whom I loved more than life itself.

Despite the long journey and frequently missing school altogether due to a series of train strikes and bad weather, I breezed through eight O levels and then studied for A levels in maths, further maths and physics. I had a natural ability for maths, passing the A level when I was only 16, and found it much less bother than remembering dates in history or quotes for English essays. My parents were adamant that I should do a degree but I didn't really have any strong idea of what to study. No one in my family had ever been to university and I didn't have any real idea of what it entailed or how to choose a course. So I plumped for a subject, the one right at the top of the list issued by the admissions council: Astrophysics. That sounded suitably mathematical and had the very satisfactory effect of nonplussing the nuns who were more used to girls who did English, French and history A levels and then trained as teachers.

My school, although good and academic, didn't prepare girls for the Oxbridge entrance exams. And to be honest Oxford and Cambridge didn't really impinge on my consciousness at all. I was more than happy to win a place at University College London, which sounded much more fun than being stuck in some dusty provincial town. When I discovered that University College was set up by the reformer Jeremy Bentham in 1828, primarily for Jews and Catholics – and later women – who couldn't study at the Oxbridge colleges, that was a plus, too.

But the course was hard, much harder than I expected. Being really, really good at sums at a nice convent school left me ill-prepared for the rigours of a tough science degree at one of the top universities. My facility for maths meant I coped, more or less, with the theoretical side but I struggled with the lab work – having done nothing more practical than embroidery at school. And it didn't help that there were only nine women in an intake of more than 100 freshers in the Astronomy and Physics department. As I saw it I was an alien among all the swotty boys. I hated it and begged my parents to allow me to leave and get a job. But they were adamant. They knew the hardship of getting your education later in life and I wasn't going to suffer as they did.

In desperation I signed up to work on the student newspaper, *Pi*, and discovered the wonderful cloak of invisibility that being a professional observer can confer. Suddenly I was right in the heart of the student union, able to go anywhere, talk to anyone, with my new-found status as a member of 'the press'. The whole panoply that was student life in the Seventies opened up to me. I attended student union meetings where we railed against the Government and passed motions to send telegrams of support to striking workers all over Britain; to Palestinians on the West Bank, and the oppressed, whoever and wherever we thought they were. Although that could vary according to who you spoke to. In student politics in the Seventies there were at least half a dozen different left-ist groupings all fighting among themselves.

The Socialist Workers Party hated the Marxists, who loathed the various types of Communists, and everyone thought the National Organisation of Labour Students exceedingly dull. Union meetings frequently went on for hours with amendments to the substantive and endless points of order and information. Digby Jones, later director general of the CBI but then a law student, was seemingly the only Tory in the College and he would heckle everyone and everything. In my guise as a reporter I moved freely among all the left-wing groups and duly wrote up reports of union meetings and Anti-Nazi League marches. As my confidence grew I took part in silent protests against apartheid and joined the occupation of the University of London Senate House complaining about – I can't remember what. Probably grants, which were universal in those days – although means tested – and we didn't have to pay tuition fees so we really didn't know when we were well off. I had a high old time at the National Union of Students conference in Blackpool where I took the stage as a speaker, glamorous in my usual outfit at the time of skin-tight jeans (I had to lie down to do them up) teamed with silky 1930s blouses bought from charity shops and high, strappy sandals worn with stripy socks. The diary pages of *The Guardian* reported that three different good-looking student activists – a Communist, a Marxist and a plain old Socialist – vied for my attentions, and according to the bartender in the Imperial Hotel we out-drank every other political grouping who'd ever stayed there.

Passing my exams became something I did to stay involved in my wonderful, radical left-wing student life – and I did so sufficiently well to be offered jobs in the defence industry, literally as a rocket scientist, during the annual 'milk round' in the Third Year. This was in the days of the Cold War and no way was I going to be part of the arms race. Journalism was a much more noble calling. The *Daily Mirror* in those days was a campaigning, radical tabloid, far more politically correct than *The Guardian* in that it was aimed at the 'workers' rather than the intellectuals. I set off for Plymouth full of high ideals and aspirations, and in John met someone who was even more principled and idealistic than I was myself.

He relished the role of observer rather than participant even more than me, to the extent of remaining deliberately vague about his background. Even though John's father lived just an hour away in Exeter, I didn't meet him for the whole of the first year. His siblings were all compulsive travellers: his brother Michael was in Israel and his sisters were in Jersey and Australia respectively. To me, with 13 first cousins and countless second cousins, it seemed unfathomable not to have a bothersome family who were always calling you and visiting you. But John's mother had apparently died of leukaemia when he was 13, or so – I never knew the exact date. And the family seemed to find comfort in travelling the world, from being apart rather than together. Having such young parents, no one in my family had died. Both sets of grandparents were still alive so this was my first experience of the impact of grief and I was astonished. Surely the death of a family member would make you want to cling together? Apparently not. With hindsight I can see that the pain of remembering can be so great as to compel you to forge a new and different life.

John had been born in Leeds and always referred to himself as a Yorkshireman, although he had grown up in Exeter. And I believe, although I'm not sure, that he was sent to the Catholic boarding school Stonyhurst, in Lancashire, around the time of his mother's illness. It seemed to me that learning to be apart from his family at that time gave him a distance that was his means of coping for the rest of his life. He started a university course in economics but chucked it in favour of a drama course in Bristol which he endured for six weeks, then left when he was asked to 'be a tree'. He then spent a couple of years indulging the family passion for travel, mainly in Canada where he worked on a fruit farm and in Israel where he lived on a kibbutz.

At the age of 21 lack of money forced him to return home to live with his father who had moved to the West Country to work for Clarks, the shoe manufacturers. From there John began firing off job applications to all the local papers, looking for work as a trainee reporter. Though he didn't know it most of the titles belonged to the Mirror Group and six of his letters found their way to the desk of the training scheme manager who, impressed by his persistence, decided to give him a chance.

The idea behind the *Mirror*'s purchase of West of England Newspapers was that while studying for our National Council for the Training of Journalists (NCTJ) exams, the trainees would provide the staff of the local newspapers. So we were duly assigned to attend council meetings and magistrates' courts and write up wedding reports. In the summer of 1979 we both transferred to the Mirror Group's regional Sunday paper, the *Sunday Independent*, which was based in Plymouth and circulated throughout Devon and Cornwall and as far into Somerset as Taunton. I was given my own column to write – Lindsay

Nicholson's Showbiz Scene, which involved interviewing anyone remotely famous who came to the West Country. I went on location with actors Charlotte Cornwell and John Thaw, interviewed Ian Lavender from *Dad's Army* when he appeared at the Hoe Theatre and waylaid comedian Norman Vaughan whom I spotted in the street. I even managed to wangle a meeting with Wayne Sleep who was merely visiting his parents who lived in Plymouth. It meant I got free tickets for all the pantos and summer shows, which was just about the only entertainment John and I could afford, and writing features made me much happier than ferreting out news stories, which was never a particular strength of mine although I did once get a scoop when the entire cast of *Joseph And The Amazing Technicolor Dreamcoat* went down with food poisoning after the first night party.

For John, though, frustrated by writing stories about missing supermarket trolleys and school students who spent their dinner money in the local café, it was the chance at last to spread his wings, as he set about uncovering building plots on tainted land and all manner of other local misdeeds. The colourful Plymouth MP Alan Clark was a regular subject of John's investigations, culminating in an exposé of a letter he had signed inviting local businessmen to join a luncheon club and contribute to party funds in return for 'jumping the queue' over certain constituency matters. Clark was forced to admit publicly that he was a hypocrite and ever after that was John's sworn enemy.

In his spare time John was also working on what was to be his first really big story – an exposé of the brutal regime imposed by some of the prison staff against prisoners on E Wing at Dartmoor Prison. This was way beyond the scope of what 22-year-old trainee reporters were supposed to be doing and senior staff on the paper warned him he'd never bring it off. Undeterred, he worked on the story on his days off, visiting Dartmoor inmates who had since been transferred to other prisons. One former lifer who had recently been released spent weekends with us at our Plymouth flat as John debriefed him about life in Chokey, as E Wing was called.

The resulting dossier was deemed too much of a legal minefield for a provincial Sunday paper to be able to print. Frustrated, on 12 December 1979 John wrote a memo to the news editor:

> It is now five months since I first heard that men were being ill-treated at Dartmoor Prison. It is two months since my investigations were completed. I have to know when we are going to use it. The way things are going I can't see that it will be used before Christmas because this is the season of good cheer and joy and we wouldn't want to burden our readers with this kind of story – or some other totally ridiculous reason . . . I feel it is my duty to make sure this story is known and I must know whether the *Sunday Independent* is going to publish it or not, now.

A compromise was reached. The *Sunday Independent* would publish in conjunction with the *Sunday Mirror*, making use of the national paper's legal firepower. It was the front-page splash in both papers and picked up by the *Daily Mirror* the following day bringing John to the attention of the legendary Fleet Street figure Dan Ferrari, then head of investigations at the *Mirror*, who was to prove himself one of John's biggest supporters, helping him get a job on the *Daily Mirror* when he'd finished his training.

John sent local MP Janet Fookes a copy of his complete dossier and she raised a question in the House of Commons which led to Home Secretary William Whitelaw ordering an investigation. But best of all, in John's view, was that he received his first death threat. We were living in a tiny bedsit on the Barbican in Plymouth and didn't even have a phone so the message was scribbled on paper and shoved through our front door. I was panic stricken but John believed that unless you were getting death threats you weren't doing your job properly.

∞

For the final part of my training I was posted to the *Daily Record* in Glasgow. John, as a non-graduate, was left behind in the West Country to do an extra six months on the *Sunday Independent* before he could be assigned to a national paper. We missed each other dreadfully and would phone every night – John calling from a phone box on Plymouth Hoe as we still didn't have a phone in our flat. He also wrote me long, long letters several times a week, pouring out his love for me and his ambitions as a journalist in equal quantities. I have kept them all. One read:

> When I turned on the radio this morning and heard about the ridiculous killing of John Lennon, I felt more than ever that we have to do something important and never become a rusting little part of all the crap. If we write, maybe at least we can tell people things or show things or something. First: I want to love you deeper and forever. Second: I want to have a beautiful life with you. Third: I want never to forget important things we have to be concerned with.

And in another he wrote:

> I want the greatest job in journalism – whatever that is. But over and well above all that I don't

want to work forever on one thing. I don't want
us to be apart. I want to have a beautiful life with
you.

Whenever I could get time off we would spend the weekend together: I would travel down overnight on the sleeper
train and we would fall into one another's arms. During
these visits, I met up with some new friends John had
made among the trainees. Like us, Alastair Campbell and
Fiona Millar had fallen in love virtually at the start of
their training and were living together. And like us, their
passion for journalism mirrored their passion for each
other. We became an inseparable foursome, united in our
belief that we could make the world a better place.

   After six months of fretting about being left behind
in the West Country, John's greatest wish came true. He
was given a placement on the *Daily Mirror*. There was no
guarantee that this would lead to a job as we were what
was known as indentured trainees, which absolved the
Mirror from any responsibility to employ us once we'd
completed our two years. So when his placement was
finished John simply stayed on, hanging around Fleet
Street working shifts whenever they were offered. I was
doing the same in Glasgow until finally John landed a
full-time job as a reporter on the *Mirror*, and I chucked
the job I'd found working for Radio Clyde and rushed
back to London to be with him in a bedsit flat we rented
in Earls Court. I found a job on *Woman's Own*, having
been confirmed in my belief that hard news was not for
me by being sent out to doorstep families of murder
victims while in Glasgow.

∞

We were married in the summer of 1981 at Chelsea Town
Hall when John was 24 and I had just turned 25. It was

at the height of the New Romantic fashion and I wore satin knickerbockers and a billowing white shirt which I'd trimmed myself with lace. Although both of us were Catholics and believers, we both disagreed with many of the teachings of the Church and were far too principled to start our lives together on any sort of false premise. After a party in the garden of my parents' house we went on honeymoon to the Greek island of Paros, but we were so broke we had to smuggle food from the market up to our room each evening as we couldn't even afford to eat dinner in a taverna. Not that we cared. We had each other – that was all that mattered.

∞

John as the youngest and most junior reporter in the news-room – at least until Alastair Campbell's arrival a few months later – was assigned the most basic jobs and despite the support of Dan Ferrari was not given leave to pursue the major investigations, which was where his real interests lay. So, as he had on the *Sunday Independent*, he simply worked on his own stories during his days off. Which meant in practice that he worked nearly all the time.

Late in 1982 an intruder, Michael Fagan, sensationally broke into Buckingham Palace and made his way to the Queen's bedroom where he sat on her bed. John had a hunch that Buckingham Palace security was lax and this wasn't a one-off breach. Together with a photographer, he obtained a security pass for the Royal Mews – where John had his photo taken waving from a royal ceremonial coach. His story 'How I Smashed Security At Buckingham Palace' made the front page of the *Daily Mirror* on 3 November 1982, and prompted a letter from his former trainers in Plymouth:

As you can imagine, everyone down here was knocked out by your story on Buckingham Palace Security. I don't think I have ever seen such an enormous byline, and certainly never on a front page.

It was the turning point in his career at the *Mirror* as, having proved himself, he was allowed to work on investigations rather than the diary stories issued by the newsdesk, which bored him. In 1983 he turned 26 and made what was to be the first of many trips to the North West Frontier on the borders of Pakistan and Afghanistan, to report on the opium harvest, following the trail through to heroin addicts in British cities. During the election in 1983 he was assigned to follow Margaret Thatcher on the campaign trail leading to her landslide victory. But politics of any colour bored him. He was far more interested in posing as a buyer for a foreign government, exposing a British firm that exploited a loophole in the law to sell leg irons and shackles overseas.

By this time I was working for the glossy magazine *Honey* as beauty editor. Carol Sarler, the editor, had been given free rein to reinvent the young women's magazine as a much more radical magazine for a new breed of independent-minded feminist. Despite my title I was never required to report on the latest make-up colours or hairstyles; rather I was allowed to carry out my own investigations into the new health-related vision of beauty that was taking over from the old warpaint and hairspray. I wrote about the new aerobic exercise classes that Jane Fonda was popularising, and studied Pilates, a full 20 years before it became mainstream. In what was regarded as magazine heresy at the time, since a tan was still regarded as a status symbol, I tracked down dermatologists who were linking sunbathing with skin cancer. It was stimulating and rewarding, and not at all arduous, for someone who knew how to investigate a story properly.

John and I bought our first home, a flat in Belsize Park, and Alastair and Fiona, who had joined the *Daily Express*, moved into another one a few doors along. Just as I had been fortunate enough to have been a student in the radical Seventies, I found myself in the heart of the media during the high-rolling Eighties. It was a high-octane and heady existence. After work John and Ali would go to the *Mirror* pub, known as the Stab In The Back. There they claimed they would drink as many as 24 pints each, on occasion – and I never saw any reason to disbelieve them. Fiona and I would meet them there and we would all go on for dinner with more wine. Or more likely champagne. We never, ever cooked at home. Fiona and I replaced our student wardrobes of jeans with chic outfits from the newly opened Nicole Farhi shop in Hampstead, and our holidays consisted of driving down through France to the coast in our company cars, stopping off in little towns *en route* to take our fill of French provincial food. We spent money without thinking about it, oblivious that these good days could ever end.

In 1984 we were on holiday outside Nice when we heard that Robert Maxwell had bought the Mirror Group and temporarily stopped all the paycheques, leaving us with literally no money in our accounts. Fortunately Alastair always travelled with his bagpipes so he and John went busking among tourists, returning to our hotel in St Paul de Vence with a hat full of one franc coins with which we paid the bill.

Back at work, scoop followed scoop as John pursued his own investigations, following his obsession with the drug trade, the arms business and the activities of the National Front. But the *Mirror* was changing and, although we didn't realise it, so were our lives. Alastair was getting more involved in politics and was made a lobby reporter in 1985. Later that year both John and Ali were offered jobs on Eddie Shah's new venture, *Today*. Neither would have considered it previously but Robert Maxwell's ownership of the *Mirror* bothered them both and they thought he was ruining its serious campaigning stance. They amused themselves by placing prank calls to Robert Maxwell's house during dinner parties and it didn't help that John had placed a fake dog turd outside the executive lift while Maxwell was entertaining Jim Callaghan. An inquiry was ordered but although John was suspected it was never proven. Even so, after much in-decision John decided to stay at the *Mirror*. Alastair went to *Today* as news editor of the Sunday edition where they were so short of staff he ended up not only running the news desk but reporting on stories, too.

Although both were too proud to admit it John's refusal to accompany Alastair to *Today* did cause a rift between them and our regular nights as a foursome petered out. In any case, John and I were having our own difficulties. Under the new regime John's investigations were wound down and he was reassigned to the routine stories, reduced to spending so much time hanging around on doorsteps trying to get quotes that Maxwell maliciously christened him Milk Bottle Merritt. Undeterred he returned to his previous gameplan of simply working on his days off on the stuff that interested him. We spent little time together and I was dreadfully, dreadfully lonely. My dream job at *Honey* had gone sour after Carol was fired and I was told by the publishers to return to the regular beauty beat of lipstick and fragrance launches in order to pull in more advertising. I would finish work at five and, having few close friends, would come home to spend the evening waiting for John's return, which would be some time in the small hours – if at all. I was 28 with no children, bored, unhappy and lonely in my marriage. I wanted a new life while I was still young. I didn't want to wait until I was tied down by children or too old to leave. The way I saw it, my childhood had been overshadowed by my father's career. I had no intention of allowing history to repeat itself.

Eventually I walked out of the marriage and my home – to the utter horror of my family for whom separation or divorce were an anathema. I went to live with Terry Tavner, a friend I'd met on *Honey*, staying in her spare bedroom, and embarked on an affair with a freelance writer who was kind and funny and attentive, but eventually broke off our relationship saying I was clearly still in love with my husband.

I didn't know it at the time because we weren't speaking, but Robert Maxwell had felt so guilty about his treatment of John that he agreed to him taking six weeks off to go and sit on a beach by the Indian Ocean and review his priorities. One day, not long after he got back, I was in a cab on my way back to the office after a very long lunch at a smart restaurant, and I felt ill. Suddenly my six-month temper tantrum evaporated and all I wanted was to be at home with John. I told the cab driver to divert to Belsize Park and I let myself into the flat with the key I still kept, and crept into bed.

John arrived home several hours later to find me there, fully dressed and fast asleep. We talked for hours and he promised he had changed. He would take at least one day off per week and be home by nine other than in exceptional circumstances. We would get a bigger house with a garden where I could have a dog and a cat, maybe even children. It wasn't so much to ask for and John stuck to his promise – more or less. We never spoke of my defection again. That was how we were. We never talked about the bad stuff. Although the guilt of it was to haunt me in the years to come.

Alastair was working even longer hours than John at this stage. I tried to resume my friendship with Fiona but she seemed distracted and unhappy about Alastair's moods and his excessive drinking. Then in March 1986 I tried to call her but was told that she and her father Bob were on a plane to Scotland where Alastair had caused some sort of drink-fuelled scene while covering the Labour Spring Conference. What happened next was frightening and very confusing – so much so that when Ali got back home and was recovering, John went round to visit him taking a bag of marbles he'd bought at a toy shop. 'Here you are,' he said handing them to Ali: 'Don't lose them again.'

Chastened by his experience, Ali never drank again. And John, although he would still drink wine with meals, had already cut out the after-work socialising. Our mad, carefree existence at an end, both couples moved out of our respective flats to houses where we could start families. Alastair and Fiona went to nearby Gospel Oak while John and I moved to a big Edwardian house in Crouch End. There was an overgrown garden which John set about landscaping and filling with flowers and herbs. For my thirtieth birthday he planted basil seeds which he carefully nurtured and then harvested to make home-made pesto sauce for spaghetti – absolutely my favourite meal at the time. After our champagne-fuelled lifestyle it was a cool and sober approach to a new phase of our lives.

In 1987, seeing no hope of the *Mirror* returning to its campaigning roots, John finally left and joined *The Observer*. Given the scope of a broadsheet, serious paper of liberal values he was in his natural element. Within a month of his arrival there he had leaked an official report which attacked British Telecom as the worst public service in Britain at that time; exposed a group of businessmen profiteering from homeless families in a Heathrow bed and breakfast hostel patrolled by security guards with dogs; disclosed how a Middlesex couple lost to the legal system most of the £30,000 damages for negligence that killed their daughter; and saved a Kurdish refugee from deportation and almost certain death in Iran. Within a short space of time he was appointed chief investigative reporter, a title he professed to despise, because, he would say: 'All journalism should be investigative.'

I was happier at work, too, having joined the German-owned company Gruner + Jahr who were launching a new weekly magazine in Britain. *Best* was quite unlike anything previously seen on the women's market and the first issue sold over 1.5 million copies, far outselling those two leviathans *Woman* and *Woman's Own*. I was hired as features editor and made such a success of the role that I was soon offered a promotion to assistant editor, which was snatched back from me when the management discovered I was pregnant. Legally, they were perfectly entitled to do this in those days but I was naturally furious and resolved to quit as soon as the baby was born. I would work freelance from home instead, I decided.

∞

John was intensely moved and thrilled by my pregnancy and wrote many letters to the baby with the intention of compiling them into a dossier for him or her to read in adulthood. One began:

> Dear Nipper, I've tried to write this story for you many times and there is a lot more to say and much more that I can't say because it would need a life-time. This story won't be corrected or published in a normal way because it is me talking to you, not carefully selected thoughts designed to impress.
>
> I tried to begin it before, months ago, when

you were just a few weeks inside your mother and she was very sick with you. It was a morning in the Spring and I was on the platform waiting for a train having just kissed your mother goodbye for the day and I was feeling great love for her and wished that day we were not going to be apart because of working and I wanted to hold her, go back and kiss her again and be sure she knew how much I loved her.

I started to tell you how brave your mother is, how beautiful and how you must know that mysteries like the making of your new life can have unmysterious effects like throwing up and feeling awful.

On the practical side, however, we were less competent. Apart from an exquisite designer outfit that John bought in France we had no baby clothes. Eventually my mother dragged me, heavily pregnant, to Brent Cross shopping centre and made me buy a buggy, 12 Babygros and a bag of disposable nappies. The natural childbirth classes reduced me and John to fits of giggles, yet we had a blithe confidence that parenthood would come naturally to us and made no plans. We didn't even discuss names. If the baby turned out to be a girl I secretly wanted to call her Eleanor. It was the name of my great-grandmother – an indomitable East End matriarch who took in washing to make ends meet. It seemed to me that Eleanor was a name for strong women: Eleanor Roosevelt; Eleanor of Aquitaine . . . But I was under the impression that John didn't like it.

On 1 December 1988, with only 10 days to go until my due date, I was still working on *Best*. I came home late from the contributors' Christmas party and in bed we started bickering about names. I asked John what exactly was wrong with the name Eleanor and he protested he'd always loved it but didn't think I liked it. So Eleanor it was. Assuming she was a girl. And as if she'd been waiting until that was settled, my waters broke the next morning all over the kitchen floor and she was on her way.

We drove excitedly to University College Hospital – with me sitting on a bin liner because of the waters – saying over and over again: 'Our baby's birthday will be 2 December.' But Eleanor had other ideas. I was in labour for more than 30 hours, and while I breathed through the contractions, John, who was bored, worked on his story for Sunday's paper about a member of the IRA. A motorcycle messenger came not only to the hospital but right into the labour room to pick up his handwritten copy.

I progressed from pethidine to an epidural to double top-ups of epidural as the pain relief was only working on one side. Eleanor was finally born at around 2.20pm on Saturday 3 December 1988. She weighed 8lb 2oz, had a dusting of fine gold hair and rose-bud lips. Weeping John took her in his arms and said: 'I'm glad she's a girl. She'll be a friend for you.'

The baby's name was quickly shortened to Ellie and if we'd given no thought before she was born as to how we would cope, we were thrown in the deep end afterwards. For the first three months of her life Ellie suffered terribly from colic. I don't think anyone really knows what causes colic. It's completely harmless but results in painful wind as the immature digestive system learns to digest milk. Every day from 2pm to 10pm Ellie would draw her legs up to her chest and scream. Only walking her up and down seemed to bring relief. When she was six weeks old John went to Sri Lanka to report on the cause of the Tamil Tigers and, at my wits' end, I took Ellie down to my parents' house so we could all take turns in endlessly walking her up and down.

When John returned, I came back home, and in an

attempt to resume our pre-baby life, John invited the photographer who'd been with him on the trip over to supper. Roger Hutchings arrived with his then girlfriend, a petite blonde girl he referred to as Hel. Ellie was still crying non-stop and I was so overwhelmed by coping with her that I'd forgotten to buy any food. There was no indication that I might one day edit a magazine known for its glossy dinner party menus. And if Hel, whose actual name was Helen Fielding, was formulating any of the witty observations on 'smug marrieds' for which her alter ego Bridget Jones became so famous years later, then she gave no sign of it, simply looking on in stunned silence as I struggled with my baby and tried to phone for a takeaway.

Magically at three months Ellie's colic disappeared and she was transformed into the sweetest, most agreeable baby – so cherubic that passersby would stop me in the street when I took her out in her pram. With the help of a Swedish au pair called Siv to mind her I embarked on my freelance career writing for the *Sunday Times* and *Marie Claire* among others, while John produced some of his finest work for *The Observer*. He was obsessed by the investigation into the Lockerbie disaster, which had happened only three weeks after Ellie's birth, and he travelled ceaselessly working on that and other stories, often unable to make contact with home. In August of 1989 he wrote to his then nine-month-old daughter:

Dear Nipper, I'm wiring this to you from Pakistan because you can't get phone calls yet. The President – a general and dictator called Zia al Haq – has been killed and I have interviewed the person who will become the new leader – Benazir Bhutto. If she's still around when you read this letter, and you want to know, she is not a great intelligence. But she is pretty and has support because of her father who was Prime

Minister and hanged by Zia. I have to write 1500 words for the paper but I could have said just what I told you.

From Pakistan he went on to Greece where he had heard reports that mental patients were being kept in appalling conditions on a remote island. His report ran in *The Observer* on 10 September 1989, and even with time has lost none of its power to shock.

The smell hits like a reek of an abattoir and the scenes flicker past like some depraved peep show.

Everywhere are prison bars. In an upstairs cell, bodies lie on beds, naked or wrapped in grey sacking material. Some are curled together finding comfort in mutual foetal positions. Not people but one being. How old are they? 28? 60?

A blanket pulled back shows knotted legs. How long has he been there? '24 years.' In the bed? 'Yes, since four years old.' Others are tied hand and foot to their beds. Why? 'To stop them from falling.'

The buildings have numbers. We enter number 16. A peeling grey-green barrack block outside a wire pen, rusting iron and rubbish. These are the ones they call 'the naked'. Filth and excrement on the walls, on their naked bodies. Some are hosed like cattle. A blind man, or one who would not see, is on the floor, trampled, defecating. Why are they here like this? 'They are the worst.'

John was denounced in the Greek parliament and his revelations were blamed for the delay in Greece joining the EC. But the Leros inmates were rehoused in more humane conditions and I was immensely proud of my husband. Of course, his travelling left me on my own again but I knew now that I couldn't live without him. If I ever felt it was hard for me being at home with a tiny baby then I only had to read about what he was doing to believe that the greater good was served by his work. Not only that but I knew he was driven by the desire to make things right in the world in which his child lived. And there was an element, too, that he didn't think he had much time. His mother had died in her forties. He knew that opportunities must be seized with both hands or they could be snuffed out.

Chapter Two

∞

IF THIS IS AS HARD
AS IT GETS?

Despite being parents our lives still continued to be dominated by the news agenda. On 2 August 1990, Iraqi troops overran the neighbouring state of Kuwait under the orders of President Saddam Hussein of Iraq and within hours John was on his way out to Amman to report on the build-up of British and American troops in the Gulf. Although he had travelled frequently since Ellie was born this was the longest he had ever been away, which threw up a problem we hadn't encountered before.

We had been together 12 years but had never thought to have a joint bank account as I had always earned my own money and we split everything down the middle. But now that I was freelance, and barely working two days a week, my own income was tiny. Within about three weeks I had exhausted the funds in my bank account and then started running up supermarket bills on my credit cards. Soon I was down to one last card – my Marks & Spencer charge card. We ate well but as they didn't sell nappies the logical choice – to me – seemed to be to potty-train Ellie, who was 18 months old at the time – a little on the young side.

John arrived back in September for a break and I took Ellie to meet him at Heathrow. All the time he'd been away I had pointed to aeroplanes in the sky and explained that Daddy had gone in an aeroplane and would soon be coming back in one. So after we'd met up with him I insisted we took her up to the observation terrace between Terminals 1 and 2 to see planes taking off and landing. But John seemed impossibly tired and could barely make the walk there. Stubbornly, I forced us on, Ellie running ahead, me trotting after her, and John dragging his kit bag along in our wake. He had planned to be home for a fortnight and first on his list of things to do was fix up a joint bank account as we thought that a war in the Gulf could well start any day and he would be away for even longer. He also went to the doctor about his extreme tiredness and nose bleed that had lasted for four days.

∞

Leukaemia is not hard to diagnose. A couple of blood tests. A trip to the local hospital. Referrals to various specialists ending up at the Hammersmith Hospital in West London. People ask how I felt when I found out. It's like asking how I'd feel if I was hit around the head with a large blunt instrument – too busy reeling from the impact to focus on feelings. Did I ever think: Why us? No, actually I didn't. Not then, nor ever over the course of John's illness and what followed. I think it's a cliché to suppose that anyone does think: Why me? Horrible things happen – you only have to look at a newspaper or turn on a TV to know that. There was no reason why my family should be immune. But sometimes I caught myself feeling . . . well, the only word is 'surprised'. I had always regarded myself as a lucky person.

There are many different types of leukaemia. John's was diagnosed as AML or acute myeloid. Not the easiest kind to treat. It's sometimes curable with chemotherapy alone but more usually requires a bone marrow transplant. One consultant John saw before ending up at the Hammersmith tried to console him by telling him that leukaemia was one of the more merciful cancers to get: it weakens your immune system so much that you get carried off by pneumonia or some other opportunistic infection! Well it may be true and it was certainly tactless, but we refused to accept that John's illness could be terminal. We just thought it was one of those hard things in life that had to be got through. And we never doubted that we had it within us to get through it. I remember, though, asking my mother how she'd coped when my father developed testicular cancer in his thirties. I focused on getting through it, she said. The alternative with three young children and no career was too terrible to think about. And so it was for me.

∞

John didn't return to Amman. Instead he was booked into the Hammersmith to start chemotherapy. On the morning of his first treatment, I went out and got us all croissants for breakfast. They tasted awful. We sat trying to force them down − me in tears because I wanted it to be a special breakfast, at which John pointed out that no break-fast on the morning you start chemo could ever be regarded as really delicious. Then he drove himself off to hospital.

Was it connected to John's mother's death from leukaemia when he was a boy? Certainly not, said the doctors. Leukaemia − like the vast majority of cancers − isn't hereditary. It's one of the most common cancers in young people and the official verdict was that lightning can, and does, strike twice. John, however, believed that the high levels of radon gas leaking from underground rocks in the part of the West Country where he grew up were to blame. He never deviated from this belief.

Before the chemo could be administered John was fitted with a Hickman line, a catheter in his chest that fed straight into a major blood vessel, avoiding the pain of constant injections, the risk of infection and collapsed veins. But the Hickman line itself is uncomfortable. John couldn't wear sweaters as they rubbed so I bought him some cardigans to wear instead. Along with the pyjamas he needed for his hospital stay, he said they made him, at 33, feel like an old man. And he had to keep the line taped up while he had a bath or a shower. Nor could he do his regular 100 lengths a day of the local Park Road swimming pool.

Today the Hammersmith has a wonderful designated leukaemia unit installed, thanks in the main to the fundraising of the Leuka charity, but at that point, despite the fact that it was a world-class unit with pre-eminent haematologists, the conditions on the wards were ghastly.

∞

John was on the haematology ward known as B3. My memory of it at that time was that it was filthy with over-flowing bins, and staffed mainly by agency nurses who had no specialist knowledge of haematology. As well as leukaemia patients on chemotherapy, this was where inmates from nearby Wormwood Scrubs were treated, the more violent ones guarded in their beds by prison officers. There were quite a few drug addicts on the ward, too, who used to shoot up in the smoking room. Those with Hickman lines used to inject straight into the lines. The others – their veins wrecked by years of abuse – used to shoot up in the only undamaged veins they had left, in their groins. And there were many of the so-called care-in-the-community cases who stayed there because there was nowhere else for them to go.

A diary John kept at the time was later printed in *The Observer*. Here's one extract from 7 November 1990:

> Hooked up to chemo and antibiotics for 18 hours.
> Shaky emaciated old lunatic Mr Moody in bed
> opposite takes his pyjamas off and pees over floor,
> hobbles towards me and tries to climb in my bed
> . . . Night-time: Mr Moody is swearing and yelling,
> 'They are trying to kill me.' Man in bed behind is
> being sick. Old man in next bed is sitting on his
> bed covered in excrement. The smell is appalling.

It was no way to treat any seriously ill person, let alone
someone with very little immunity from infection. I was
dogged about visiting every day, usually having to take
Ellie with me. Since John didn't trust hospital food, I often
drove there with a plate of home-cooked food balanced
on the passenger seat beside me. While John ate, I chased
Ellie as she toddled down the ward and took her repeat-
edly to the filthy toilets as I was still potty-training her.
Actually, I was toilet-training her as I realised I could
hardly walk around a hospital ward (even if I did doubt
its cleanliness) with a potty in a carrier bag.

And I was still trying to work on a freelance basis. My
cousin De came to stay with us to provide back-up for
John after our daily nanny – always known as Nanny Su
– went home. We put De on the insurance for John's car
so she could drive over to the Hammersmith to collect
John after his chemo. Unfortunately, De had been living
abroad and was used to driving on the right.

On one of the first trips she made she hit a police
motorcyclist and knocked him off his bike. He was fine
about it and said it was probably his fault (was he really
a policeman?) so we didn't bother to tell John. A week
later she was involved in another collision and the bumper
pinged off John's Golf. Undeterred she picked it up off
the road and put it on the back seat where – needless to
say – it was the first thing John spotted as he got in the
car. 'Oops, I was hoping you wouldn't see that until later,'

she said, when he challenged her. After that John decided it was easier to drive himself.

After eight hours of chemotherapy every day John's glorious golden hair came out in handfuls. Everyone I have ever known who has had chemo has felt most bitterly the loss of the hair. The nausea, the discomfort, even the fear that it might not beat the cancer, are feelings that all come and go but the baldness is there every time you look in the mirror. It's the ultimate indignity. John refused to go the baseball cap route, let alone wear a wig. Instead he invested in a large brown felt fedora which he wore for work, substituting it with a tweed cap at weekends.

During a brief respite between chemotherapy treatments in early 1991 John's own bone marrow was harvested (an operation done under general anaesthetic and involving drilling about a dozen holes into the pelvis) but as he was never really well, it was never of sufficient quality to be of any use. In any case, at that point what are known as autologous transplants were in their infancy. And had not been proved to be particularly successful. John's brother Michael in Israel, and both his sisters, Anne and Jane, by now living in Australia, had blood tests to see if they could donate their bone marrow. We were quite hopeful at that point because there is a one in four chance of matching with a sibling. But it was not to be.

I pinned my hopes on the Anthony Nolan Bone Marrow Register set up in 1974 by Shirley Nolan when her young son Anthony needed a bone marrow transplant. Anthony didn't survive but thanks to her drive and initiative there are hundreds of thousands of volunteer donors on the register and nearly 500 transplants are performed every year in Britain alone. But, again, the numbers didn't work in our favour. John didn't match with anyone on the Anthony Nolan database nor with any of the other similar databases that have since been set up around the world. We had to do this privately as the NHS wouldn't pay so we spent thousands of pounds on fruitless searches – no one matched. Unless someone new came on the database we would have to rely on chemotherapy alone. Or a miracle.

Although John spent as little time in hospital as he could wangle, inevitably there were times when he couldn't avoid it. Bored and disgusted by conditions on the dreaded B3, he amused himself by exploring the corridors, usually dragging his drip trolley along with him. This was how he discovered a brand new, unopened ward. What's more it was a designated ward for people who were immune-suppressed and needed barrier nursing – specifically those with AIDS or leukaemia. It was made up of individual rooms each with an ante-room where medical staff and visitors could scrub up before entering.

Back on B3 John called the hospital administrator from the ward phone and invited him down to explain why conditions there were so awful, yet there was a brand-new, unused purpose-built ward just a couple of floors away. In the story that appeared in *The Observer* on 4 November 1990, he revealed that the ward had been built by private donations but there was insufficient NHS money to open it. The ensuing rumpus ensured that it was indeed opened, even though half the beds were reserved for private patients in order to fund it. But at least John was one of the first patients to move in.

It made an immeasurable difference to be nursed under proper barrier conditions. At last John could relax, not thinking he was going to catch something from another patient or the filthy floor. An extra bonus was that we had a measure of privacy when I visited, and the amount of trouble Ellie could get into in just one room was limited.

However, a bed on B5 wasn't guaranteed. Whenever John or any other NHS patient with AIDS-related illnesses or leukaemia was admitted, they had to take their chances on which ward they were sent to. On one of the few occasions that John referred to the possibility of his dying, he asked me to ensure that he died at home or on B5, not on the loathed B3 with the addicts and the prisoners. As it turned out I wasn't able to do that for him.

Even when he had a bed on B5 John was reluctant to spend a minute longer than necessary in hospital. If his chemo was timed to run overnight he would drive home again in the morning. If he felt well enough he would drive to the office. He was usually immune-suppressed either because of the chemo or due to the leukaemia itself which meant he had to avoid anyone with a cold or flu, or worse. He couldn't use public transport or go to public places. He also had to be very careful about what he ate, sticking to what we referred to as the 1950s diet. Unpeeled fruit was out, so was salad, unpasteurised cheese, mayonnaise, lightly cooked eggs, pâté, chilled convenience meals, rare meat, and barbecued food; more or less our entire diet in our previous lives. Vegetables had to be thoroughly boiled. Meat overcooked. Fried food was even safer than boiled because fat heats up to a higher temperature.

Eating out was a nightmare except, bizarrely, for fry-ups in greasy spoon cafes. Worse was eating at friends' houses. However much I tried to explain beforehand, I would see a cat jump onto a work surface or the same utensils used for cooked food after raw meat and signal to John not to swallow anything. I tried to brief friends before we went anywhere but if you haven't ever experienced catering for someone who's immune-suppressed it can be hard to get your head around what matters and what doesn't. Before our visits to my parents, my mother would clean and polish, vacuuming the house until the pile on the carpet all but wore away. But then she would unthinkingly use the same tea towel two days running.

We could have taken food prepared at home for John but he hated any special measures so usually he just wouldn't eat and I would choke down double quantities out of politeness. In my own home I could be fanatical about cleanliness, and I was, despite a barely potty-trained toddler and a dog (why didn't I send the dog to live with my mother? I suppose because I didn't see why leukaemia should deprive us of all the pleasures in life). At that time I became quite obsessive, preparing whole meals and then throwing them away because I couldn't be sure that I'd scrubbed all the work surfaces thoroughly enough before starting.

Once I became so hysterical that I plunged my hands into a bowl of neat bleach in a desperate attempt to destroy any lurking bacteria. I scrubbed my hands so often they became raw and chapped. Then I worried about bacteria lurking in the cracked skin. If there was anyone I could have turned to for advice in this period, I never knew it. I still don't. I just cleaned and scrubbed and cooked and cared for Ellie and tried to make everything in our home as nice and as safe as I could for John. Trying to blank the horrors from my mind.

∞

One day on my way to visit him in hospital, I passed something that seemed barely human being wheeled back to the ward. Bald, naked except for a sheet, horribly emaciated, breathing through an oxygen mask and with tubes coming out of the chest. It took me a full few seconds before I grasped that this was my husband. John, however, was stoical about the pain, and the indignity. Primo Levi was his favourite author and he read his books about concentration camps and the Holocaust over and over again. Once I found him reading the *Lonely Planet Guide to India* and I was so surprised I asked him what he was doing. Surely he wasn't thinking of going there? 'I'm allowed to dream still, aren't I,' he snapped. Most of the time, however, his eyes remained firmly fixed on the higher ground, believing that man's inhumanity to man is a far greater evil than the simple fact of biology that means human beings get ill and die.

He rarely lost his temper and never complained even when, during a period of steroid therapy, he had to inject himself in the stomach every morning, something I couldn't even watch so he'd do it out of my sight. If he possibly could – and this was most days – he'd go to work, driving himself from North London to the *Observer* offices in Battersea. On breaks between chemo he would insist on the Hickman line being removed so that he could start swimming again. He never sought refuge in self-pity and didn't even go back to drinking, usually sticking to tomato juice when out with other journalists.

In fact, he was so good and strong that I felt like the repository for all the bad, crappy thoughts. Sometimes, when I was driving somewhere, I'd fantasise about just putting my foot down and driving away from it all for ever. Just going somewhere far away with Ellie and starting a new life under a new name. But most of the time I knew that as hard as this part was, things would get immeasurably harder if (when?) John died. And there would come a time when I would bitterly regret every mean word or distant moment between us. So I did what I could to diminish the impact of his illness on our lives.

∞

I started visiting different churches and praying for his recovery. During this period I became obsessed with the idea that we weren't married in the eyes of God. I wanted us to be together for eternity not just our mortal lives. It bothered me terribly that although we were both Catholic we had only been married in a register office, and I wanted our marriage blessed by the Church. That sounds like it ought to be simple but it's not. We consulted the priest who had baptised Ellie – an expert in canon law. He told us that rectification of marriage (the technical term) could be viewed with suspicion by the Church as it can be used by bigamists. There was so much red tape to be sorted out that I felt defeated by the enormity of it all.

One Sunday night I was especially tearful about it so John went around to the presbytery of the local Catholic church, St Peter in Chains, in Stroud Green. It was only five minutes away but, typically, as I always do things the complicated way round, it was not one of the churches I'd been visiting. He was gone for hours. When he finally got back he was very drunk but I managed to get out of him that he'd fixed it for the marriage to be blessed. Apparently he'd rung the doorbell and it had been answered by Fr Anthony Maggs CRL who was the local parish priest. John blurted out what he'd come about, Anthony invited him in, poured him a whisky and they sat and talked for four hours. I never knew what they talked about but for John it was a significant turning point and Anthony became his spiritual guide through his darkest moments. Sometimes John would joke about it, saying it was like something out of a book and that he believed if he'd gone back the next night a very elderly housekeeper would have opened the door and said, 'No, there's no Fr Anthony here but there used to be 100 years ago . . .'

Anyway this Fr Anthony was real enough and within a few weeks he had sorted all the paperwork needed for our blessing. On 1 May 1991 John and I remarried with Ellie as bridesmaid, my friend Terry as matron of honour and Mike McCarthy, an old friend from the *Mirror*, as best man. John and I both look awful in the pictures. John's hair had grown back after chemo into a sort of brown, dog-like brush and he's too thin for his suit. I didn't have time to shop and am in an ill-fitting cream linen top and an old blue Marks & Spencer skirt that I wore for work. I carried a bunch of cream roses bought in the local florists. Ellie looks cute though in a dress I bought specially and Terry took a picture of her swinging on mine and John's arms as we made our way down the aisle. Afterwards we all went to an Italian restaurant in Crouch End and had wedding cake made of Tiramisu.

It was a tenet of faith for both of us that we should continue to live as normal a life as possible. We had friends over for dinner and visited them in return. On 5 November 1991, just over a year after John's diagnosis, we went for dinner at Mike McCarthy's flat in Crouch End. We were going to watch the Alexandra Palace fireworks from his balcony so I took Ellie. Fiona was there, too, with her children Rory and Calum and it was the first time we had met Mike's pregnant girlfriend, the journalist Jo Revill. Mike had moved to *The Times* as environment correspondent. He'd met Jo (who was also covering the environment then) at a conference and their relationship had developed very quickly.

John and Alastair were extremely late, which was not unusual for them. When at last they arrived they were full of the news that Robert Maxwell had disappeared over the side of his yacht. Not only that but Alastair, who was then political editor of the *Mirror*, had heard it while in the press room at the House of Commons. Michael White of *The Guardian* had joked, 'Bob, Bob, Bobbing along,' and Ali had punched him.

At the time, this seemed to us an entirely reasonable response. We knew Robert Maxwell was not a nice man – very few press barons are. We'd all suffered at his hands and we knew he'd driven the Mirror Group into debt. What nobody knew at that point was that he'd taken money from the pension funds – the pension funds of nearly everyone present at the dinner that night – in a desperate attempt to keep the company afloat. But it seemed to us then that to make fun of someone's death –

however much you dislike them – was in poor taste. Alastair's reaction might have been over the top. Indeed, when he later became famous the incident was often used to indicate an aggressive nature. It is, I think, to Alastair's credit that he has never since sought to justify his over-reaction by explaining that he was on his way to spend an evening with his best friend who was dying.

In any case, we never discussed the fact that John was dying. Ever! Looking back, it seems bizarre that not only did John and I not discuss it, we never even discussed what my financial situation would be in the event that he didn't pull through. Not only bizarre but irresponsible. The reason, of course, was that neither of us could bear it. And, to be fair to John, he would have been reassured that I would be eligible for a widow's pension from *The Observer* and that the mortgage on our house would be paid off. But I actually didn't know that. And I never dared to ask what Ellie and I would live on after he died. I think we both assumed that I would carry on working but I'd already been turned down for a job with my old employers Gruner + Jahr on the magazine *Best* because of John's state of health. (Yes, the same people who took away my promotion when they found out I was pregnant – you'd think I'd have got the hint.) My freelance work had dwindled away to virtually nothing. I found it harder and harder to motivate myself to work. To be honest I was losing my nerve, too. Pitching ideas to commissioning editors, ringing up total strangers and asking them for interviews, and then finally submitting your article only – usually – to have it sent back for revisions, all take a kind of confidence that I could no longer muster.

In early 1992 John was found to be in remission but, even so, he still had to go to hospital once a week and I would stare for hours out of the window of the bedroom that served as my study, fretting until he rang me with the results of his blood count. They never got any better.

Often they were worse. Then on the days when he was at work rather than at the hospital it would seem mean for me to work, too, when I could be playing with Ellie or making a meal for his return. We may not have discussed the future but I knew that our time together as a family was precious.

Then, on Terry's recommendation, I got a call from Judith Hall, the editor of *Woman's Weekly*, asking me to cover the features editor's maternity leave. She took me for a welcome and very long lunch at Joe Allen's in Covent Garden where I managed, through a haze of alcohol, to negotiate a three-day-a-week deal ostensibly so I could carry on with my other freelance work but really because I couldn't commit any more of myself than that.

It wasn't the most cutting-edge place to work for sure. *Woman's Weekly* had the oldest and most conservative readership, by far, of any of the mainstream weeklies. It even featured a cheesy cartoon serial about a family of robins, which Judith had tried to get rid of when she took over as editor but had to reinstate after a concerted campaign by the readers. There were a rock solid half million of them which meant *Woman's Weekly* was a haven of calm in the often uncertain world of the IPC weekly titles. Most of the staff had been there for decades. There was a fully staffed kitchen which provided cakes for all occasions and food to take home for the weekend and even a knitting department with three full-time knitters! Going into work three mornings a week was like entering a warm bath.

As features editor my duties were light. Each week I would commission some human interest pieces and a celebrity profile – this usually from Richard Barber who had recently parted from *OK!* magazine where he had been launch editor. There was no one he didn't know or couldn't get to, so his work flowed in effortlessly and on time. The department secretary was a young girl called Julie Breck and I used to let her fix up all the pictures. She would call up top name photographers like Alan Olley and Sven Arnstein and arrange for the major photoshoots as calmly and efficiently as she made the tea and opened the post. I was happy to give her as much responsibility as she could handle and she has since made a great career in magazines, most recently as editor of *Family Circle* and *Essentials*.

After I'd been there a few weeks, Eileen McCarroll, the features editor, gave birth to her baby – or rather three of them. She had been expecting triplets but not dared tell anyone for fear of what might go wrong. Obviously they were very tiny when they were born but as soon as we were sure they were going to make it Judith asked me to interview Eileen for a piece in the magazine.

But I had a secret too and it was that I was pregnant. John was the only other person who knew. From the moment Ellie was born I had wanted more children. Since her birth we hadn't used any contraception but nothing had happened so when John was diagnosed 18 months previously we didn't think it would. Although it seemed only fair to let Nature have a chance.

All my life I'd disagreed vehemently with the Catholic Church's standing on contraception but with my new-found interest in religion it suited me to go along with the view that all life is precious and to stand in the way of its creation is wrong. I'm sure some people think that if you are terminally ill sex is the last thing on your mind. In fact, I would say, the reverse is true – it can become a celebration of life.

I interviewed Eileen on the Friday but over the weekend noticed a brownish discharge. By the Monday I was bleeding heavily and went to my GP who sent me straight up to the Whittington Hospital in Highgate. I took a taxi there as John had bronchitis and in any case couldn't leave Ellie. So I lay alone on a trolley in A&E for three hours, waiting for a bed, while my precious chance of another child ebbed away. I had nothing to read and no one to talk to so I fished in my handbag and found my notebook with 90 minutes' worth of shorthand notes from my interview with Eileen about the successful arrival of her three babies so I passed the time transcribing them.

Finally I had a scan which showed I'd had an incomplete miscarriage, and was admitted to a ward overnight in order to have a D&C in the morning. I begged the doctors just to give the baby a chance. With Eileen's story fresh in my mind I thought maybe it was twins, or even triplets, and one could have survived. But they told me there was no doubt and I'd get gangrene if they didn't get rid of the foetal matter left behind.

I was put on an antenatal ward and each patient had a sign above her bed stating what she was in for, written in acronym form to preserve our privacy. I can't remember what my sign read — something about evacuation of womb contents. But it didn't take me more than a minute to work out what S.T.O.P. above most of the beds stood for. With crashing lack of sensitivity the Whittington Hospital had put women in for abortions, or Selective Termination of Pregnancy, in beds alongside women having miscarriages. I was alone as they wheeled me down to theatre in the morning and as the anaesthetic started to take effect I was crying: Don't take my baby. When I came round there was a nurse with me who hugged me and told me I could try for another baby after three months. If only.

I went back to work on *Woman's Weekly* on the Wednesday without even having to take a day's sick leave, and submitted my copy without telling anyone where I'd been when I wrote it up. Even my mother who'd come up to help John cope with Ellie while I was in hospital thought she must have misheard and that I couldn't possibly have been pregnant — although she didn't ask what I was in hospital for. We are a family who don't ask questions if we don't want to know the answers.

So our baby was mourned only by John and myself. We wrote the dates he (I was sure it was a boy) was conceived, and lost, on the back of a wooden crucifix which hangs above the kitchen door. And John wrote me a card. It read:

> Lindsay, My mind seems very tired. I feel bad that I've given you this problem. I feel bad that I haven't given us our son. I feel bad that I don't seem able to give you what you need. I feel bad and angry with myself in so many different ways and I've been taking it out on you and that makes me feel worse. I'm sorry. Love

More than 10 years later when I wrote about my experiences in *The Guardian*, many of the hundreds of people who wrote to me were grieving after a miscarriage. Each of them without fail prefaced the letter by saying they knew it wasn't the same as losing a child. It's not. But it is, I know for a fact, utterly devastating. It is the loss of hope. And that's why John and I decided then that in the unlikely event of us ever having another child and if it were a girl she would be called Hope. But it seemed as if there would never be another baby.

∞

Without ever really discussing with John the reason why, I accepted a job as practicals editor of *Woman*. It was – and is – a big-selling weekly magazine, also in the IPC stable, but my salary was only £26,000; even in 1992 that was less than I'd previously been earning but I felt that if I was in a job I would at least be able to apply for other jobs from that position of strength. In May before I started my new job we went on holiday, driving through France, John, Ellie and myself, accompanied by our lovely Nanny Su, and stayed in a villa in St Tropez before heading back again via Paris and the newly opened EuroDisney.

As always, John did all the driving because I'm sort of dyslexic about telling right from left so can't really drive very safely on what I persist in calling the wrong side of the road. We had no medical cover and John had been fighting leukaemia for 20 months at that point, so God only knows how he managed it. But he stayed well throughout.

Ellie aged three was Minnie Mouse crazy and we got her a pair of Mouse ears and headed off for the Park so she could meet Minnie Mouse for real. But as we walked in the Park she whipped off her ears and refused to approach Minnie who was signing autographs. John was upset that the Disney moment was spoiled and it was only afterwards we realised that when she was wearing the ears she actually thought she was Minnie and to see the Mouse herself destroyed that illusion. Even at the age of three Ellie's imagination could overwhelm her.

I started work at *Woman* when we got back. David Durman was the maverick and hugely talented editor. He gathered around him a team of fiercely ambitious journalists he called his Tufty Club and let them scrap it out, until he felt like picking over the remains and choosing what were the best ideas to go in the magazine. It was a fantastically successful system and *Woman* was going from strength to strength, overtaking for the first time ever its stable mate and closest rival *Woman's Own*. In his Tufty Club at that point were Keith Kendrick who went on to edit *Loaded* and Carole Russell who later took over from David as editor and took *Woman* on to even greater heights.

I was in charge of the Fashion, Beauty, Homes, Gardening, Cookery, Competitions and Offers departments and my first shock on Day One was that 14 of my staff had been made redundant the previous week and I had precisely nine people to generate all those pages. Terry was editing *Chat*, another weekly magazine owned by IPC, and every morning she would pick me up and drive me to work as I sobbed uncontrollably at the thought of John's deteriorating health, leaving Ellie and facing another day of struggling to meet David's impossible demands with fewer than half the staff I was expecting. As she drove I wadded tissues up under my eyes so that my mascara didn't run down my cheeks. I would still be whimpering as I got out of the car, went through reception and got into the lift; but as I walked into the open plan office and was greeted by my few remaining staff, running up to me with proof pages that needed to be sent to press, stories of shoots that had gone wrong, and copy that needed rewrites, I discovered for the first time the blessed relief of working so hard you don't have time to think of anything else.

There was only one problem. I had an insatiable appetite for carbohydrate in all forms and would eat at my desk all day long. Eventually, half-believing, I did a pregnancy test one morning (while stuffing a packet of digestive biscuits into my face with the other hand). It was positive. I was pregnant again. John and I did a mini war dance around the kitchen but could not possibly believe this baby, conceived in his state of health, could survive. We didn't tell a soul. John had relapsed and his options for treatment by this time were limited. The intense chemo was obviously a busted flush. He was put on a very mild form of chemo and weekly blood transfusions to keep him ticking over while we continued to search databases all over the world in the hope that a suitable bone marrow donor had come onto their books.

In the meantime he became very interested in alternative therapies and stayed twice at the Bristol Cancer Centre where he learned to meditate and revised his diet to include massive amounts of vegetables including a kilo of carrots juiced every day. Did it extend his lifespan by even one day? I suspect not. Did it make him feel better during the days he had left? Absolutely!

The hypnotherapy, especially, gave him the resources to deal with the interminable boredom of treatment. At least once a week he would drive himself off to the Hammersmith for a day as an outpatient. He would take with him a copy of the *Daily Telegraph* and a tiny radio with an earpiece. The veins in his arms were gone and, as he refused to have another hated Hickman line put in, they would do the blood tests and deliver blood transfusions into the veins in his feet. He would spend the day reading the *Telegraph* from cover to cover, doing the crossword, listening to Radio 4 and meditating.

The long periods of low immunity had led to the aspergillus fungus colonising his lungs, which made him very weak and vulnerable. He would frequently cough up round rubbery bits of lung tissue. On more than one occasion he coughed so hard that he cracked a rib. But at least his hair had finally grown back and in its original colour. He looked more normal than he had for well over a year. I think I believed we could go on like this indefinitely.

∞

Meanwhile, even though we weren't telling anyone else I thought I'd better confess to my GP that I was pregnant. She was stunned, but laughed and said she'd had her suspicions. I went for my initial check-up at the hospital and a nurse took mine and John's medical history, and then asked: 'So, do you want it?' A little taken aback, I said I did so then she shook her head and noting my age

— 35 — said I should at least have tests for Down's. I explained that I didn't want the tests as I would never terminate this baby. So there I was half naked on the examination table and she called in a doctor who gave me the hard sell for the Down's testing, saying that even if I didn't want to terminate, it would be better to know what I was in for.

Well, this was in 1992 in the days before the internet made it possible for everyone to look up medical information — but one of the joys of being a journalist was access to all sorts of medical journals that came into our offices. I'd recently seen a medical paper saying that precisely the opposite is true and that parents cope much better when presented with a live child, however great its disability, rather than fearing during pregnancy that they might be carrying some sort of monster. So I flung that at the doctor, chapter and verse, heaved myself off the examination couch, pulled on my clothes and flounced out, never to return. Which was fine except now I had no hospital to deliver this baby assuming it survived. Luckily a friend of Terry's, Angus McIndoe, came to the rescue and got me into St Mary's, Paddington, where they arranged for me always to have antenatal appointments before the clinics started so I didn't have to sit with other mums with more certain futures. John and I went there for my first scan and that was the only time John ever saw our baby, waving her arms at us — our tiny flicker of Hope.

With the danger of miscarriage over and actually having seen our baby, we decided to start telling people. Most were very shocked, especially one of John's doctors, which annoyed me as he was the one who had assured us that leukaemia wasn't hereditary. I had only been in my job at *Woman* for four months and I was four months pregnant. It was to be several years before legislation was introduced safeguarding the jobs of women who discovered they were pregnant shortly after starting a new job so it was with some trepidation that I approached David Durman. David didn't have children himself so I wasn't entirely sure how he would take the news. As it turned out he asked just one question – do you want to come back here afterwards? Despite how awful those first few weeks had been I said yes. I'd stopped crying every morning and was actually relishing the challenge of the job and the fact that it left me no time to think. David didn't have the power to grant me maternity leave but he said he would have my case put before the IPC Board. A few days later he chased me down the corridor, caught me and gave me a big hug. The Board had agreed to give me 20 weeks' paid maternity leave – an astonishingly generous gesture given that legally they owed me nothing. I hugged David and began to feel that things might just possibly turn out okay.

∞

At the beginning of August, two years after his diagnosis, John seemed to achieve some sort of inner peace. He rang his father in Exeter and his sisters, and had long chats with them. He made appointments for lunch with all his friends. One day I was drawing money from a cash point near my office when a car drew up and a Greek god got out, walked over to me and kissed me. It was John. He had been to lunch with Alastair and was driving back to the office. I remember the sunlight on his hair – he was so golden and beautiful. We stood there snogging like school kids. I kept thinking how bloody lucky I was to have married him.

For my thirty-sixth birthday on 7 August 1992, he took Ellie and me to see the ballet Coppelia at the Royal Festival Hall. Ellie had developed an obsession with feathers and sat in her seat conducting the music with a feather she'd found. In the interval we went out onto the balcony and saw London pigeons flying about the twilight, lit up by the lamps on the South Bank so they looked as though their feathers were tipped with gold. Over the years I've been to the South Bank on many occasions but never seen that before or since.

By that time all John's hair had grown back and he had no scabs, sores or obvious signs of illness. The chemo tablets made him vomit a lot but his weight was reasonable and he didn't look emaciated. He went to work nearly every day and one morning in August as we were having a cuddle in bed prior to getting up he said to me: 'I don't think I'll live to see this baby.' I said nothing. It was the only time he'd ever spoken about dying. I remember lying very still wondering how on earth to respond. Then he said: 'You'd better get up now if you want a lift into work.' I let out a gasp. 'You can't say that to me,' I said. 'You can't tell me you're going to die and then offer me a lift to work. You can say one or the other but not both.' He laughed and the moment passed. We never discussed it again.

On Saturday 15 August, John went into work as usual. He did some work following up leads on the Rachel Nickell story. She had been murdered in broad daylight on Wimbledon Common in front of her two-year-old child. Meanwhile I drove over with Ellie to see my cousin Sue and her daughter Zoe who was also three years old. We took them to Victoria Park and both children had ice creams. Far more went on their clothes than could ever have been in the cones.

That night John wasn't too well. He was vomiting a lot and we assumed it was from the chemotherapy drugs. But he rallied in the morning and we drove out to Essex to my parents' house as they were having a swimming party. On the way John was terribly tired and thirsty. He got in the back seat of the car and lay with his head in

Ellie's lap. 'I'll look after you, Daddy,' she said. He was so thirsty I had to stop at a service station to buy him a can of drink which he glugged down in one go. At one point he said to me: 'Do you believe in an after life?' I was driving but I gestured at the motorway, the traffic, the industrial estates. 'I don't believe that there's all *this* then just nothing,' was the best I could manage.

My mother had hired the swimming pool in the school next door as a belated birthday celebration for me and invited over some guests to swim and then have dinner. John had brought his swimming things, of course – he loved to swim – but didn't feel like it when we got there and said he'd rest instead. I swam with Ellie then helped my mother get the dinner but John still didn't come downstairs. I could feel yet another trip to the hospital coming on. And on a Sunday evening as well. I didn't fancy explaining John's state of health in an unfamiliar A&E department, so I asked my mother if we could leave Ellie with her and head back to London. Getting a sleeping child out of bed to make a small hours dash across London to hospital was something I'd done a few times and didn't particularly relish.

By the time we got back to London John was better and insisting he didn't need to go to hospital. So we went to bed. I had only been asleep for about an hour when I awoke to the sounds of John crashing about on the landing and groaning in pain. I got up but couldn't work out what was wrong with him. It seemed to be some sort of intense pain in his hip that stopped him being able to walk. I had no idea what could be wrong with him. He didn't know either and kept bellowing at me: 'What's happening, why can't I walk?' 'I don't know, I don't know,' I cried over and over again. 'I'm not a doctor. Let me take you to the hospital. They'll know.'

John would only agree to go to the hospital in absolute extremis but eventually he relented. I pulled on the track pants and striped sweatshirt I kept for our not infrequent late-night dashes and headed out to start the car. John followed but his legs gave way and he fell over in the road. I tried to lift him up but he was too heavy for me and didn't seem able to use one of his legs. I shouted at him, terrified that another car would come along and run us both over, and somehow he got up and threw himself into the back of the car – stretched out full length across the seat – and I drove to the Hammersmith. It was about one in the morning and I parked in an ambulance bay near the door as I knew I'd never get him from the car park into the hospital. As it was I had to pull him out of the car and then he fell over again, taking me with him so I was pinned underneath him. Medical staff came running out, thinking we were drunk and having some kind of fight. But luckily they recognised John and got him onto a stretcher and into the A&E department. By the time they examined him they found one buttock swollen and black. He had been haemorrhaging into his hip which was why he couldn't walk and why he was so thirsty.

He was admitted back onto Ward B3, given trans-fusions of blood and platelets (to help clotting) and put on a morphine drip which I turned up to the maximum although it did little to alleviate the pain. John lay face down on the bed, in extreme pain but still conscious and talking, even making jokes. I just sat and stroked his shoulder and told him over and over again how much I loved him.

As dawn broke on Monday 17 August, I felt my spirits lift a little. Things always seem better in the daylight. John was dozing lightly so I walked down to the chapel and prayed for a bit, then bought a copy of the *Daily Telegraph* in the hospital shop to take back to the ward and read to him. I rang my mother to see how Ellie was and said I'd come and collect her later. I'd have to take a day off work anyway as I'd had no sleep.

I went back up to the ward and as I approached John's bed he looked up and smiled at me. I remember being struck by how blue his eyes were. Then, as if in slow motion, I saw what I hadn't taken in before, that there were doctors and nurses running and flinging back the curtains and bringing the crash trolley. A nurse grabbed me from behind and started to drag me away backwards. I kept my eyes locked on John's. 'I love you,' I called out and he returned my gaze until I was pulled out of sight.

I sat in the visitors' room with a nurse. What can I do, I wanted to know. We could try praying, she said. So we prayed. I prayed as hard as I could that this was just another one of those scares. And we'd lived through so many already. But after about 20 minutes the doctor came into the room. 'It's bad news,' he said. But that wasn't good enough for me – I wanted it spelled out. 'If he's dead, tell me he's dead,' I said. So they did.

Then they took me back to sit with him.

I'd never seen a dead body before. He didn't look as if he was just asleep but he didn't look as if he'd gone either. I sat with him and stroked his shoulder as I had through the night and it seemed to me that his spirit finally left as I sat there.

Then the curtains were drawn back and my brother Jeremy was there. 'Oh Lins,' he said. 'I've come to take you home.'

Chapter Three

∞

JUST TELL ME, AM
I GOING MAD?

Jeremy drove me home. I felt too sick and giddy to stand up so I crawled into bed and lay there. The world had been blown off its axis and I had to cling to the side of the bed for fear of falling.

Some time passed and then the door opened and Ellie came in. What do you tell a three-year-old about death? I didn't know. Another of the many things I hadn't thought through. I pulled her into bed with me and just said: 'Daddy's died. He's gone to Heaven.' I was crying and Ellie started crying too. And then the baby kicked for the first time. Not just a flutter but a really hard kick – the first I'd felt.

We lay there crying for what seemed like hours but it was still only mid-afternoon, so I asked Ellie what she wanted to do and she said she wanted a Princess Bride My Little Pony. So we got up and went downstairs where my mother was waiting and all got in the car. We drove to Woolworth's and bought a Princess Bride My Little Pony, which is a white toy pony about four inches high with a long flowing mane and tail and a veil. And I thought it was wonderful that such a little thing could bring some comfort – however momentarily.

Walking back along Crouch End Broadway we passed a group of three or four people. From their faces I could see they were in great distress although they were making no sound and one of them – a woman – was clutching a grey plastic bag marked 'Patient's Property'. I realised that they were probably in the same situation as me – or one very like it. And I knew then that I must have seen deeply grieving people on the streets on so many other occasions and never even noticed. But now I was one of them – the living dead – and despite the fact that I felt as if I was being torn apart with pain, it was all on the inside and completely invisible to the world at large.

In the evening my cousins Sue and De came to look after me and we watched a film. They cooked me an omelette which I couldn't eat and although I was desperately tired – having had no sleep the night before – I didn't want to go to bed. All the time I stayed awake it was still Monday 17 August 1992, the last day on which John was alive. When I woke up the next morning it would be the start of the days when he wasn't.

But Tuesday came flooding into my bedroom with a burst of glorious August sunshine. The world continued to turn even though John was dead. How could that be? I would have stayed in bed but downstairs there were noises of activity and people coming and going. After our day's grace yesterday this was the start of that surreal time that exists between a death and a funeral. In later years I discovered that this period of heightened reality with so many duties to perform is actually enshrined in many major religions. But I had no idea what to expect then. I knew nothing of anything. I was 36 but had only previously been to two funerals. The first dead person I'd seen was my own husband.

The doorbell was ringing. It barely stopped ringing for the next 10 days. Flowers were arriving. Bouquet after bouquet of flowers. I put the first ones in vases, but I quickly used up all the vases. Then I moved on to buckets, then the sink. I was fast running out of space. My mother and my Aunt Jo turned up and threw themselves into a flower-arranging frenzy using Oasis foam to fix flowers into any and every container they could lay their hands on. They even wove flowers through the fireguards in the living room. Some of the bouquets had been beautiful but they ended up as a jumble of clashing colours and the smell was overpowering. Seemingly as the last bloom was fixed into place the first ones were dying and I was left mopping up pollen and dead leaves and throwing out bowls of rancid water.

And the post came, bringing with it a slew of letters. I knew nothing of the etiquette of death. I had never before received – or to my shame sent – a letter of condolence. I started to read them although I could barely see through the mist of tears. Friends wrote. Some just a line or two. Others sent pages. Susan Edwards quoted a passage from *Dr Zhivago* that I found especially comforting then and still do:

> You are anxious about whether you will rise from the dead, but you have risen already – you rose from the dead when you were born and you didn't notice it . . . However far back you go in your memory, it is always in some external, active manifestation of yourself that you come across your identity – in the work of your hands, in your family, in other people . . . This is what your consciousness has breathed and lived on and enjoyed throughout your life. Your soul, your immortality, your life in others. And what now? You have always been in others. And what does it matter to you if later on it is called your memory? This will be you – the real you that enters the future and becomes a part of it.

John's colleagues from *The Observer* and the *Mirror* wrote telling me anecdotes about his work life that I hadn't heard before. And there were many, many more letters from people I'd never even met. Those John had helped through his various investigations including nearly all of the Lockerbie families who said how grateful they were that John had pursued their case despite his own worsening health.

In total about 400 letters arrived over the next few days and I read every single one of them. Apparently you are supposed to reply to letters of condolence but I didn't know that. And I couldn't have done it anyway. There were too many and each one reduced me to a puddle of emotion. I just parcelled them up in four box files for Ellie and the new baby to read when they were older.

And the phone kept ringing with people who wanted to know how it had happened, how was I? How was Ellie? And there were yet more flowers. And I had to call my office and sort out some of the things that needed my attention and there was Ellie to get up and dress and care for.

In the midst of all this my brother Jeremy arrived and said we must make a start on the funeral arrangements. What? I wasn't ready. I'd barely absorbed the news that John was dead. Jeremy was gentle but firm although to my knowledge he'd no more experience of these things than I had. There are things you have to do, he said. But I couldn't. So – luckily – he did.

John had made few plans for his death. His papers were most definitely not in order which pleased me in a way as I didn't want to think of him spending his final days on Earth filing all his paperwork. Although I did think he might have done a little bit at some point in his life! We had a tiny boxroom that was his study and his system was simply to chuck any and all bits of paperwork into it. He may have started putting papers on his desk but over the years – and long before he got ill – the mess had grown so bad that he could barely open the door. Which left Jeremy and me with it all to sort out.

So I sat on the floor and went through the papers one by one filling plastic bin bags with rubbish. It was a bit like being on an archaeological dig and it was several days before I got down to 1987, the year the study window blew in. Although the glass was replaced, John had left the shattered panes where they lay and they had been covered over with paperwork in the intervening five years. And there was still more paperwork underneath that.

One of the things he *had* done though was to destroy most of the diaries I knew he had kept during his illness as if he didn't want me to know later on how much he'd suffered. I longed for a last message from him but all I found among the credit card receipts and notes about stories he was working on was a last scribbled note to Ellie:

> Nipper – Sometimes you'll forget what I look like.
> That's OK. The thoughts, love, feelings I have felt
> will live on in you.

It took me about six full days to get down to the floor and there was no choice but to do it because our finances were in a terrible mess and death is expensive. Despite being on a good salary, John was overdrawn because he was owed hundreds of pounds in work expenses which he hadn't bothered to claim. Not that it actually mattered that he was overdrawn because our joint account had been frozen immediately the bank was notified of his death, so I had no means of accessing any money anyway. It was unfrozen two weeks later but during that time I'd had to pay for the funeral and settle John's Barclaycard bill My diary records that I rang my bank for a £2,000 overdraft on the Friday then upped it to £5,000 the following week.

Thank goodness I had my own account and, as of the last few months, my own small salary being paid into it as well. And thank goodness too for the death grant of

£1,000 which arrived within a couple of days and without which I could not have paid the undertakers. This benefit is only payable to widows and widowers. I realised then – as I was to realise so many times in the coming months – that the point of getting married is not that you need a piece of paper when things are going right but it certainly does help when things go wrong. Having been married also meant I was automatically eligible for a state widow's pension which, along with a pension from *The Observer*, meant I had some choices. I would have to carry on working but at least the pensions topped up my salary enough to cover my childcare costs. And I wouldn't have to sell the house.

It was hard to have to learn the lessons of financial reality when I was still in shock but I suspect I'm not the only one. If I had my time over again, the one thing I would change is that I would have got our finances on a more organised footing before John even got ill. I don't know what I would have done without Jeremy to help. As much as I tried to take responsibility myself – phoning up the bank, the mortgage company, the insurers – I would become stuck and tongue-tied when I had to explain that my husband had just died, our bank account was frozen and that's why the mortgage – or whatever – hadn't been paid. Jeremy patiently worked through calling everybody and fixing up the funeral.

Meanwhile I picked out the clothes to dress John's body: chinos, navy blazer, yellow silk tie with blue spots. It comforted me to be ironing his clothes and getting things ready for him. I sent them over to the undertakers along with a rosary we had bought when we visited the Vatican. And I wrote him a long, last love letter which I wanted to place in the coffin. I was so looking forward to seeing him again. I planned to take Ellie and to sit by his body every day until the funeral. My friend Terry wasn't keen on this idea, though. She insisted on coming with me the first time and she wouldn't let me take Ellie. I thought she was fussing. I just wanted to see my husband.

The undertaker ushered us in. I went over to the coffin. It wasn't him! I stood, stupefied. Repelled. Yes, the body was wearing his clothes but it wasn't John. Or at least technically it was – but it was nothing to do with him. The essential being, the soul that had made him John, was no longer there. Fool that I am, I'd packed a comb in case they'd done his hair differently but that was the least of it. His face without the expressions I'd known and loved for so long didn't look like him. Not even asleep. I'd so longed to see my husband one more time. But he'd gone that morning in the hospital. What was left behind was irrelevant. Just skin and bones and hair.

I managed to put my letter and a letter from Ellie, and the feather she'd found, in the coffin alongside him and I kissed his icy lips one last time. But when we got outside I was sobbing uncontrollably. He really was gone. Terry held me and comforted me and told me it was good that I'd seen him. It would make it easier to get through the funeral if I knew we weren't burying a person but simply their remains.

∞

Because it was August it was quite hard to get a date sorted. In the end, the only day that the undertakers and cemetery could both manage was 28 August – which would have been our eleventh wedding anniversary. Friends tried to talk me out of it but I felt that it was very fitting to bury my husband on the anniversary of the day I had pledged my life to him.

We arranged that he would be buried at Highgate Cemetery and Jeremy took me there for a meeting with the manager and to pick out a plot. I don't know what I expected of a cemetery manager but he wasn't creepy at all. He was a young, good-looking man and I was greatly impressed by his passion not only for the history of Highgate but also for the way it continues to provide an ever-changing memorial to the people who have lived in the area. He asked me if I wanted a single plot or a double. Double, of course! I couldn't wait to be buried alongside John. But the only plot I liked – just to the left of Karl Marx, which I thought John would appreciate – was a single.

We trailed on looking at other sites, Jeremy marching on ahead talking prices and maintenance with the manager – it's run as managed woodland rather than as neatly mown lawns – while I dawdled behind reading the gravestones. This was something John and I used to do a lot when we went for walks in the Cemetery on Sundays, always finding something new. I stopped at one I must have passed many times but never noticed before. It read: 'In memory of my beloved husband . . .' and then a Polish name, probably an airman who had died in the Second World War. But the grieving widow had obviously married again – possibly one of his friends because after the word 'husband' an 's' had been chipped in using a different typeface and another Polish name inserted underneath. Poor woman – she'd bought a double plot when the first husband died but been widowed again before she could take up her rightful place in it. How practical to pop the second husband in alongside! It tickled me to think of it and I stood there, tear-stained and laughing my head off. Jeremy thought I had become hysterical but in fact I was making my mind up. I told them the single plot would suffice. I would just have to live.

And there was yet more to do in this interminable 11 days before we could bury John. My youngest brother Hugh and his girlfriend Suzanne had been dating since they were at school together and now, after 15 years, were finally getting married. It felt as if almost 15 years of planning had gone into the wedding which John had then wrecked by dying just four days beforehand. Suzanne was distraught and wanted to cancel the wedding but no one would let her and really it was too late. In any case, Ellie was to be a bridesmaid and it seemed mean to deprive her of that pleasure, too.

Suzanne's family is German and she had designed traditional dirndls in pink silk for the bridesmaids. Ellie had been for several fittings and was beside herself with excitement. She had spend the past few weeks practising her bridesmaid walk in front of John and me. So on the Saturday after John's death, Jeremy – who was best man – drove us down to Essex for the wedding. I made it to the church, weeping throughout the ceremony, but decided not to go to the reception. My parents took Ellie on with them while I returned to their house to spend the night.

The next morning I got up at about seven to make a cup of tea. While I was doing so my mother came into the kitchen and somehow a row flared up between us. To this day I don't know what it was about. Nor I suspect does she. The only notes I can find in my diary seem to suggest it was about who had travelled with whom to the church the previous day and I can hardly believe that so much pain could have been caused by something so trivial. But neither of us was in any fit state to be rational.

My mother was not only grieving for John but for her own father as well. Albert had died earlier in the year and his wife Rose was suffering from advanced dementia. Then, just weeks before John died, my father had been diagnosed with cancer – again! He'd already had testicular cancer, then a malignant melanoma, now it was bladder cancer. This was his third diagnosis of the disease and the outlook, as ever, was grim. We were both struggling for air among the dead and dying – and both as angry as hell about it. It was a very brief but deeply bitter fight. I flounced out of the kitchen, packed our bags, woke Ellie and asked Jeremy to drive us back to London, feeling doubly abandoned because I'd not only lost my husband but – it seemed – my mother as well.

∞

The day before the funeral I went shopping for a dress to wear. At nearly five months pregnant my shape was changing daily. Nothing I owned fitted me and thanks to the cashflow problems there was no money in my bank account. By an incredible stroke of luck, I found a black silk chiffon trapeze-shaped dress in a secondhand shop in Hampstead. It was beautiful and fitted me perfectly. I dug out a black lace mantilla I'd had for years and chose a lilac printed cotton dress for Ellie.

On the day of the funeral I got us both ready and then, exhausted by the effort, lay down on the bed to wait. The doorbell rang and someone said it was time to go. John was waiting outside . . . for all the world as if to pick me up and take me to the church. Our last ever journey. I got up but I was shaking all over. How on earth was I going to get through the funeral? Once in the car though a strange calm descended over me as we followed the hearse to the church.

I had ordered 200 red roses to cover John's coffin, which was carried by his brother Mike Merritt, along with Alastair Campbell, Mike McCarthy and my brother Jeremy. Ellie and I walked behind. Fr Anthony said the requiem mass and despite being afraid that I would break down I remember feeling as if I was looking down from above, watching the terrible grief in that church. Grown men – grizzled old Fleet Street hacks – choked back sobs but my inner self looked on dispassionately as a single tear rolled down my cheek and splashed onto my shoes. At the graveside Ellie tossed her posy of freesias into the grave as the coffin was lowered. Although she was only three at the time it was something she remembered doing for the rest of her life.

Ever-faithful Terry had organised the wake. John had never discussed it but she decided that he would have wanted us to have gallons of champagne and stand about reminiscing, getting progressively drunker. So that's what we did and I had some champagne, too. It was a gloriously sunny afternoon and Ellie ran about the garden, cooed over by all the adults. As evening fell, Terry's partner Will fired up the barbecue. It was a great party. John would have loved it.

∞

With the funeral over I was at a loss to know what to do. I'd cared for John through his illness for two years and then prepared his send-off but now he no longer needed me. The only thing I could think of was to go back to work but Alastair and Fiona were adamant that two weeks wasn't long enough to recover. I needed at least another week off and they persuaded me to join them on their summer holiday. They had rented a house in the Dordogne with another couple, Carrie, a GP, and her partner Nick. The bank accounts had been unfrozen so I was able to book Ellie and myself on a flight to Toulouse. John had always made the travel arrangements for our family so I was nervous because this was the first time I'd ever bought airline tickets. Needless to say, it was completely straightforward and Alastair picked us up from the airport. As we hadn't been included in the original holiday plans there weren't enough bedrooms for all of us so Ali and Fiona gave Ellie and me their double bed, saying that because I was pregnant I should have a proper night's sleep. Fiona squeezed in with the children: Rory, then four, and Calum, three. Alastair never complained about spending every night of his summer holiday on the sofa.

In fact no one complained about the disruption to their plans. I blush now to think what terrible company I must have been, especially for Carrie and Nick whom I'd never even met before. I just remember crying most of the time or feverishly writing in my diary. I was incapable of looking after Ellie so she was just sort of rolled up into the Campbell family. At that time her favourite meal was plain pasta with a tiny bit of grated cheese – which was all Rory would eat, too – so while Nick cooked up elaborate meals for the adults, Fiona prepared plain ones for the kids. It rained incessantly but Alastair spent hours devising indoor games or reading out loud with the three children all piled into one big chair on top of him. It's my favourite mental image of him, like a big lion with tiny cubs clinging to his mane. There was a swimming pool but it was too cold for the children and most of the adults, although Fiona swam every morning – her lips blue and teeth chattering for the rest of the day.

At the end of the week the others flew home but I hadn't been able to get a flight until after the weekend so Ellie and I checked into a hotel in Toulouse. The bad weather cleared, the skies brightened, and Ellie and I spent two days exploring the beautiful rose pink city. Remembering this, I wonder that a three-year-old could have made such a great travelling companion but she did. She walked miles uncomplainingly, chose what to eat from the menu in restaurants and gravely absorbed all the sights. When we got tired we would go and sit in the dark calm of the cathedral and light long, thin candles for John. And I had a sense of liberation from knowing that no one had any idea that we were bereaved, the living dead. For 48 hours we were anonymous, not pitiable.

Back home, the Summer was over and it really was time for me to go back to work and for Ellie to start school. Walking back into the office was a blessed relief. Quite probably no one knew what to say to me but the pace of life on a weekly magazine doesn't allow much time for sitting around chatting. I flung myself back into my work, grateful for the distraction. A week or so later, I took Ellie to St Aidan's nursery school for her first day. The first of all the 'firsts' that John wouldn't see.

There was no school uniform, so to streamline our morning routine I bought her several tartan pinafores which she would wear with white rollneck sweaters underneath and navy blue tights. Each day I would drop her off at the nursery before going on to work. At not quite four, Ellie could already read, write her name and paint recognisable people and animals. She was a sociable child, too, and loved nursery, settling in quickly. I think it fulfilled the same purpose for her as work did for me – a part of her life that wasn't about death. But it was only two hours a day so it made no difference to my child-care arrangements. I still needed a full-time nanny if I was to be able to put in the long hours demanded on a big-selling weekly magazine. At 11.30 Nanny Su would pick Ellie up from nursery and look after her for the rest of the day until I got home around 7pm. Then I would cook supper, put Ellie to bed and, because I couldn't afford a cleaner as well as a nanny, I'd then do the housework from 10 to 11pm every night. I didn't mind. Despite the crushing pregnancy tiredness, I couldn't sleep.

When I was so exhausted I could no longer remain upright, I would go to bed and lie there writing in my diary and saying the prayers of the rosary until sleep overwhelmed me. Most nights I dreamed about John. Sometimes he would be trapped somewhere, maybe down a mineshaft and running out of air but I was unable to reach him. Other times I dreamed he'd come back to life.

He'd tell me he'd gone away to South America for an experimental treatment and been cured. 'I let you believe I'd died,' he'd say, 'because that way it was less painful for you.' These dreams were torture and because I was pregnant I couldn't take a sleeping tablet or an antidepressant. Nor even have a drink to help me sleep. I would have stayed awake all night if I could. But inevitably I would drop off in the small hours and the dreams would return. It was always a relief when morning came.

I had never lived alone before. From university, I'd moved into lodgings with Dilys, then set up home with John. In my exhaustion and loneliness I began to wonder about my sanity. I became obsessed with the idea that I was going mad with grief and that Ellie would be taken away from me, as would the new baby as soon as it was born. No one suggested any help. No health visitor called. The Hammersmith Hospital did not provide any sort of back-up. I went to see my GP and asked in as casual and off-hand a manner as I could muster if there was any counselling to be had. I didn't want her to see how crazy I felt. She fixed up for me to see someone for an hour a week, on Thursdays before work.

At that point I had no idea what counselling was. I just guessed it was the sort of thing that someone in my situation might need. And it was – in so far as it went. The counsellor was a kind, motherly woman, a vicar's wife. We sat in a windowless room in a church hall drinking instant coffee and she gave me the basics that everyone needs in order to understand the process of mourning, for which I am eternally grateful. I asked her if I was going mad. She told me no, I was simply experiencing the different stages of grief. These stages of the grieving process are apparently well known (although I'd never heard of them before) and were identified by the psychologist Elisabeth Kubler Ross. When you itemise them in the cold light of day they sound quite logical and rather unsurprising really.

With the news of the death comes **shock**, very real physical shock which often brings with it symptoms like nausea, vomiting and the vertiginous feelings I'd had when I clung to the side of the bed, afraid I would fall off.

Then **denial** takes over. This is when the mind refuses to accept what's happened because it's all just too enormous and too terrible to take in. It's what gets you through all the organisation necessary in those early days and explains my sense of being an observer at John's funeral. How long this phase lasts depends on a lot of things. For most of the mourners, the funeral ritual brings it home that this is real – a death has actually happened. But the closer you are to the person who died the more your mind seeks to protect you from the truth. Widows (or widowers) rarely break down and fling themselves on top of the coffin. More often they stand calmly and unemotionally in the eye of the storm while everyone around them comments – between sobs – how wonderfully well they are coping. They're not. Nor are they unfeeling. It's just that the loss is so great they simply can't take in what's happening. Denial is a blessed phase because you feel little or no pain but it doesn't last. Reality keeps breaking though.

As the fog of denial starts to clear, you begin to get glimpses of the awful, unbearable sadness. It's like having a blindfold taken off and finding yourself standing on the edge of an abyss. To save ourselves from falling into the abyss we conjure up **anger**, which is a wonderfully strong, powerful emotion that pushes out feelings of sadness – even if only momentarily. Understanding this explained the fight with my mother after Hugh's wedding which, weeks later, I was still feeling sore about. People always think that at such a time you shouldn't let petty squabbles get in the way. In fact, the reverse is true. The feelings of helplessness in the face of cruel fate are so overwhelming that the only thing that brings any relief is a good old row about something utterly incon- sequential. Every death I've ever heard of has involved at least one fight between the mourners. I think funeral directors should hand out printed cards to the bereaved warning them not to take anything that's said personally.

Flip-flopping between denial and anger keeps reality at bay for a bit but as time passes it becomes apparent that the person you loved is never, ever coming back. Then there is nothing for it but to sink into the hope- lessness of **despair**. This apparently happens anything from three months to more than 18 months from the death, so theoretically I hadn't even hit that bit yet. Except I had, I said. I would cry for hours every day, unable to stop. Crucially, my counsellor explained to me that the stages of grief don't arrive in an orderly fashion: rather they overwhelm you in waves and it's only when you look back that a pattern emerges and you see that some weeks were mostly about denial or that anger was the key to a particular series of events. At the time, though, you are simply whipsawed through a rollercoster of emotion, unable to take in what's happening. And it takes years to work through all the different stages before reaching the end goal, which is **acceptance**.

Acceptance, by the way, is as good as it gets. You never forget. You never return to the old you. You just learn to live with it. If you are lucky. I didn't think acceptance sounded like much of a reward after years of pain. And it is literally years.

For a straightforward bereavement – without belittling the pain involved, this means the death of someone older, say, who has died from natural causes – the stages of grief are generally agreed to take around four years to work through. Four long years. For a complicated bereavement – that's the death of a child or young adult, or maybe an older person but in unnatural circumstances such as an accident or even murder – then it usually takes at least seven years to work through the stages of grief. And while it's not unusual for it to take much longer, it certainly won't take any less. Nor is time the great healer on its own (whatever well-meaning friends like to suggest). It's very possible, and very common, to get stuck in one of the stages – usually depression but it can be anger – and just stay there, never moving on.

The Hollywood idea of death has the whole mourning process done and dusted in the space of a few months – max. If only . . . I totted it up. Seven years of the hard labour of grieving – and grieving is very hard work. I had just turned 34 when John became ill. I would be 43 before I could expect to feel anything like normal again. Years when other people could make strides in their career, raise their families, build up their homes, which would all be trashed for me by the rottenness of illness and grief. And I felt very, very sorry for myself. If I'd known what was to come I don't think I could have endured it.

So it was, I started obsessively counting not only the days but the hours and minutes since John's death. Ticking them off in the hope that I would reach some magic number and start on the upward path to feeling okay. But I was so far away from that. I was still going rapidly downhill.

We as a society used to know all this. We used to wear different coloured clothes to signify where we'd got to in the grieving process. Victorian women veiled themselves in deepest unrelieved black for the first year, gradually adding touches of white, then moving into lilacs and greys as they approached the magic four years. But with improved health and longevity we've forgotten all this wisdom and have to go to counsellors to understand what's going on or else we think we're going mad. I know I did.

Nor was I in a fit state to take all this new information on board. Week after week I would sit in the windowless room asking: Am I going mad? Week after week I would be told: No, this is natural. This is normal. But it didn't feel natural or normal. It felt like hell. I get so angry now when I hear people sneer about the need for counselling. But kind and loving and supportive as my friends and my family were, no one else I knew at that time had the knowledge or the experience to help me and tell me what I needed to know about the grieving process. And even my counsellor, experienced as she was, admitted that helping someone who was carrying a posthumous baby was outside of her experience. To be pregnant – literally full of life – in the very teeth of death complicates things. A lot.

I have since found little research on the subject and rarely met anyone else in the same position. But one thing I do know is that if our society is generally a little wary of the bereaved, bringing with them as they do a reminder that we are all mortal, then a pregnant widow – sex and death all rolled up into one fecund shape – breaks all the taboos.

Trying to get back to normal I went to a party about six weeks after John's death. And stood alone at one end of the room with a glass of mineral water while – it seemed – all the other guests huddled at the other end throwing nervous glances over their shoulder at me: 'You go and talk to her . . .' 'No, you . . .' In some cultures the bereaved don't socialise for anything up to a year after the death. I can quite see why.

And then there were the people, the friends – or rather former friends – who simply never spoke or wrote to me or phoned me ever again. I saw one woman in the wine bar where I'd gone for lunch with my team from work. I used to know her well and when I saw her across the bar, I waved. She looked aghast, avoided eye contact and exited as soon as she could pay her bill. Charming! But in truth I hardly cared. After all, I used to be that person – the one who didn't know what to say, so scampered out of sight in the hopes of not being spotted. I thought I would say something wrong or hurtful. I didn't know that to say nothing was far worse. What could be more cruel than to walk away from a friend who is in pain, after all? But people did it to me over and over again – too afraid of their own mortality to speak to me. To be honest, though, it really didn't matter. There was only one person I truly missed. And he was never coming back.

Was my religion any help at all? Non-believing friends of mine thought it must be. And it was. A bit. Though probably not as much as they thought. As a cradle Catholic I'd spent most of my life rebelling against the Church rather than embracing it. I disagreed emphatically with its teachings on contraception, divorce, gay rights, celibacy of the clergy, women priests and just about anything else you could think of. But . . . I did have a faith in something out there. Something bigger than all of us. Bigger than the universe itself. This had come about not through years of Catholic schooling but directly as a result of my scientific training. When I was at university one of the courses I took was cosmology, which extrapolates back to when the universe began, right after the Big Bang. And what happened before that, I'd asked the lecturers. Astrophysics is the study of what can be measured, I was told. And the time from the Big Bang onwards is measurable. Before that is religion!

So yes, I believe in something. Not in an old man with a white beard. Nor in Heaven as a sort of cocktail party where you meet up with everyone who has gone before. But I do believe. I couldn't and can't accept that the entire universe was created just so we can live out a few short years on a lump of rock spinning around a frankly rather boring star on the outer arm of a very ordinary spiral galaxy. There is, I have no doubt, more to it than that. I just don't know what.

I had not had much time for the rituals of religion when everything was going well, finding it all rather boring. As a teenager I bitterly resented being dragged out of bed to mass every Sunday morning. When everything went wrong in my life I began to find religious rites comforting, not only in that they acknowledge that there is a bigger picture but also in themselves. After all, the rites surrounding death – in whatever religion – have evolved over hundreds, or in some cases thousands, of years to help people cope. I found they were not dissimilar to what I instinctively found myself wanting to do. Praying – especially saying the rosary – is simply a form of meditation. Lighting candles helps on dark days. And the Catholic tradition of sending mass cards reassured me that people I didn't even know were going to spend an hour one Sunday thinking of my husband and our shattered family.

It also gave me a framework to explain to Ellie what was happening – without which I think I would surely have gone crazy. Or crazier. Three-year-olds don't ask one question once and are then satisfied with the answer. They ask the same question over and over and over again. In the normal world it's: Why is the sky blue? With Ellie it was: Where's my Daddy? Over and over again. Sometimes she would get furious with me, thinking I was hiding him. 'I want my Daddy,' she would scream. 'I want him NOW.' She would refuse to go to bed because she was waiting for her Daddy to tell her a story. And sometimes she would search endlessly around the house, expecting to come across him in the one room she hadn't looked in. 'He must be somewhere,' she would say. She told me that she dreamed about being able to see, touch, hug and kiss her Daddy and asked if Superman would be able to bring him back. Once my aunt Jo was showing Ellie old family photographs, explaining: 'That man's called John like your Daddy was.' 'My Daddy's still called John,' said Ellie. 'That's his name.'

It's a common fallacy that children don't grieve as adults grieve. They do but adults just can't bear to acknowledge it. The pain is too great. It's a terrible thing to see a child grieve. Naturally Ellie started sleeping in my bed again. For each of us it meant there was someone to reach out to in the night. But sometimes there was no comfort to be had. She would twiddle her hair in her fingers until she pulled it out at the roots and her movements got slower and slower. Eating a meal easily took an hour. If I tried to hurry her she would go floppy and drowsy. One Sunday when we were going to lunch with friends it took me three hours to get her up and dressed and ready to leave the house. Sometimes all I could do was wrap her in a blanket and put her in the car aiming to dress her when we arrived. I was frantic for company to distract me. She just wanted to stay at home in case her Daddy showed up.

In October, three months after John died, *The Observer* held a memorial service for him at St Bride's church in Fleet Street, traditionally the journalists' church. There were tears but it was more bearable than the funeral had been. And uplifting in that it was very much a celebration of John's life and work. The St Bride's choir sang Verdi's *Chorus of the Hebrew Slaves* in tribute to his ceaseless campaigning for the dispossessed. There was a reading from the Gerard Manley Hopkins poem which had been his mother's favourite – one of the few things he had told me about her:

> I have desired to go
> Where springs not fail
> To fields where flies no sharp and sided hail
> And a few lilies blow

Alastair gave the eulogy, his voice breaking with emotion: 'In his death he can teach us so much about how we should live and about how we should ply our trade. He never ran with the pack. He was unbeholden to any political creed or dogma. He was without cant. He was utterly fearless. Not stupid, not macho, just fearless.'

And he told the story of the time John had visited him in hospital with the marbles – the first time he had spoken of his breakdown in public.

∞

The next day I had an antenatal appointment and I arrived in a bit of a state because I'd stupidly followed the same route to St Mary's Hospital as I'd used to drive to the Hammersmith when John was a patient. Just driving along the same road made me wobbly. Then I discovered I was scheduled to have a blood test. I've always been squeamish about needles and the last time I'd had to have a blood test – when the pregnancy was confirmed – John had been with me and talked me through it, telling me to think of ice-cream to calm my feverishness. Suddenly I was plunged into a hideous flashback, all the while berating myself for being afraid of needles and the way I had only been able to stand uselessly by as my husband had literally bled to death. I fainted and had to be put in a side room for two hours to recover. The drop in my blood pressure meant that it was impossible to get the blood out of my veins and anyway I was crying and hysterical. After that the consultant agreed that we would try to get through the rest of my pregnancy without any more blood tests.

So we limped on. Ellie moving in ever slower motion. Me unable to slow down at all despite my advancing pregnancy, still working, cleaning, writing my diary and praying. I became obsessed with the idea that John was trying to send me messages. My brain simply wasn't accepting the finality of death. Surely if he loved me he would try to contact me, wherever he was? It made me a bit peculiar about phones. I left the answering machine on all the time and checked it obsessively whenever I returned home in case he had left a message. (Obviously, I never told anyone about this – not even my counsellor.) Once when I was out I passed a phone box with a ringing phone and ran to answer it, convinced it would be John.

Ellie turned four at the beginning of December. I had it all planned out and bought her a Wendy House – at least a metre square and a metre and a half high – and assembled it in the playroom after she'd gone to sleep on the night before her birthday. But during the party the next day I was overcome with grief and lay sobbing on my bed. The other mummies were desperate to know what they could do to help but I couldn't explain to them that I was crying because it was gradually sinking in that if John hadn't returned for Ellie's birthday then he must really be dead.

∞

I would have done anything to get out of Christmas. But at eight months pregnant I couldn't get on a plane and go anywhere. I just had to tough it out. Organisation was the key, I told myself, and ordered all the presents from a mail order company. But the weeks passed and no parcels arrived. Eventually on 15 December, I rang to find out what had happened. There was a delay, I was told, and the presents wouldn't be delivered now until after Christmas. A delay! It was bad enough that I'd let John die – now I was ruining Christmas, too. I cancelled the order and spent every lunch hour for the next week shopping. There were IRA bomb scares in London that winter but I lumbered in and out of shops undeterred. I couldn't bring John back but I could at least try to engender some Christmas magic.

I even managed to bring home a six-foot tree by myself and on Christmas Eve I put Ellie to bed and went down into the cellar to find the decorations. John had packed them away the previous year in an old cardboard box and as I brought it into the light I saw he had written something on it. It was his last message to us – written before he knew that I would be pregnant again. 'I love you both,' it said. And I sat on the cellar stairs and wept my heart out because at last it was sinking in that he truly had gone.

∞

Chapter Four

WHO'S ARRIVING?
WHO'S LEAVING?

Nineteen ninety-two – the last year in John's life – turned to 1993 and I was full of new life, although it didn't feel that way. I was huge and lumbering with nothing to wear. When I was pregnant the first time around I'd wanted one of those twee T-shirts that read: 'It started with a kiss', but I hadn't been able to find one anywhere. Now the shops were full of them but I didn't feel as if I could carry it off. My situation was too morbid. I was carrying a dead man's child. In mid-January I stopped work and lay like a beached whale on the sofa watching the home videos we'd made over and over again and writing in my diary.

On 28 January 1993, I had an antenatal appointment at St Mary's Hospital, Paddington. And got a parking ticket – thank you very much Westminster Council. Normally, that would have been enough to exhaust me but I was fired up with energy and in the afternoon I took Ellie up to John's grave. It was wet and muddy and at nine and a half months pregnant I was in danger of slipping over, never to get up again. We clung to each other for support and struggled back to the car covered in mud. Back home, though, I rallied and did an hour or so's gardening before it got dark. Then I wrote myself a note, which I left on the kitchen table before going to bed, to remind myself to ring the hospital about booking the pool for a water birth.

In the early hours, I woke up feeling very odd indeed. For some reason I jumped out of bed and went and stood in the bath. As I did so my waters broke and gushed over my feet. I was all alone in the house apart from Ellie who was asleep in bed yet I was curiously unperturbed. Ellie had been born more than 30 hours after my waters had broken so I didn't expect the birth to be imminent. I filled the bath with clean water and lay down in it. I felt curiously disconnected from what was going on but the warmth was good as my back was aching.

As the water cooled, I topped it up again and again but my back was still hurting. Eventually the warm water didn't ease the pain any more so I reluctantly got out of the bath and called Terry. She arrived within minutes but had to let herself into the house with her key as I was already back in the bath and refusing to get out. All I wanted to do was lie in the bath. She rang Angus, our obstetrician friend, who as bad luck would have it was on duty at a hospital in Cambridge that night, but dictated instructions over the phone. 'She's got to get out of the bath and get to hospital,' he said. I refused. 'Tell her if she doesn't get out of the bath I'm sending an ambulance for her!'

I heaved myself out of the bath. Nanny Su arrived to look after Ellie and with much muttering and groaning I allowed myself to be put in Terry's car and taken to hospital, 20 minutes' drive away. As she drove along the Marylebone Road Terry noticed that I kept catching my breath. 'You're having contractions.' 'I am not.' 'You are,' she screamed putting her foot down. 'And they are coming every 30 seconds – look at the clock on the dashboard.'

It was 6.50am when she swung the car to a halt near the hospital reception. Nurses hurried out with a wheel-chair to take me up to the ward but I refused it. My body might have been about to have a baby but my head was having none of it. Eventually they got me into the lift and along a corridor to a labour room where I was strapped to a monitor. It showed the baby was in distress – there was no heartbeat. Of course there wasn't. Now everyone would know what I'd known all along, that life couldn't come out of death. Nothing as wonderful as a baby could come out of something as terrible as John dying.

The brakes came off the bed and the double doors were flung open to rush me down the corridor for an emergency Caesarean when, with one almighty push, it was all over. The time was 7.18am – less than half an hour after we'd arrived at the hospital gates. The birth was very fast and violent. I just shut my eyes and screamed. And I kept them shut. People were telling me to open my eyes and look at the baby. I couldn't bear to because I was so certain it was dead. I waited for the cry to tell me it was alive but none came.

'Open your eyes and look,' Terry said, weeping and laughing at the same time. 'She's got John's hair. She's got unruly hair.' And there was Hope, not crying, just slowly blinking as if in recognition. Her face was a little battered where the forceps had helped her on the last bit of the journey but otherwise she was a healthy, robust 8 lb 13$\frac{1}{2}$ oz baby with – yes – unruly red hair.

She's *alive*, I said. I had been absolutely convinced that she would be born dead. How could a dead man's child live? But there she was. Only then did the miracle of her existence hit me and it overwhelmed me. I knew then that the name John and I had chosen together was so right. She was Hope. A tiny flicker of light when it seemed as if there was nothing but darkness.

I was too distressed to hold her so the midwife passed her to Terry, saying: 'You may want to sort yourself out first, though.' And we realised that in all the high drama since we'd come screeching into the hospital, Terry still had her heavy winter coat on.

The obstetrician gave me a hug and kissed the top of

my head. It felt right to be held in a man's arms, however briefly. Babies shouldn't be born into an all-female world, I thought.

∞

'You've got a sister. You've got a sister.' At home, Nanny Su woke Ellie and they danced around the bedroom together. Hope and I were fast asleep when they arrived so they had to go to the cafeteria to kill some time. Ellie asked for a Coca-Cola, which she immediately sicked up everywhere. In the excitement no one had remembered that she couldn't tolerate fizzy drinks. Finally they were allowed into my side-room and Ellie stared at baby Hope in wonderment. 'I'll always look after her,' she breathed.

The hospital had put me in a single room so I didn't have to endure the sight of all the proud fathers coming and going on the postnatal ward. But even so, just being in a hospital environment was upsetting – bringing back memories of John – and I insisted on going home. I'd lost a lot of blood. The doctors thought I should have a blood transfusion but I refused. More memories. I'd just go home and build my strength naturally, I told them.

Nanny Su was going to be there during the day and my mother and my aunt Jo were going to take it in turns to spend the nights. In truth, I didn't want anyone at all. I just wanted to be on my own with my two daughters but that was never going to happen. Everyone was concerned I was going to haemorrhage, or something, so I submitted – with extremely bad grace – to having minders for two weeks.

Most of the time I refused to get out of bed – just lying there crying and breastfeeding. Every part of me hurt. My breasts were sore and swollen as the milk came in. My stitches hurt and my wrist was sore from where a needle had been put in. Even my throat hurt from screaming so loudly during the delivery. I was anaemic from the blood loss with a haemoglobin level of 9. That was the level that John's count used to reach on a good day – after a transfusion. I was as white as the sheets on my bed and could barely sit up but John had gone to work with counts as low as 4. It made me cry even more to think about it.

I didn't want to go downstairs anyway. My mother and Aunt Jo were working hard to please me but to my mind they were mucking up my nice kitchen, using all the wrong saucepans, cooking food I didn't like and creating chaos out of my well-ordered house. In desperation, when I wouldn't eat, my Mum cooked rhubarb crumble, which had been my favourite when I was a child. She did it on one of the nights when she was at her own home and handed it over to Jo the next day to heat up in my microwave. Except Jo wasn't used to microwaves so she overheated it and with all the fat and sugar in it, it exploded. Panicking, Jo grabbed what she thought was a cloth to clear up the sticky red debris – except it was my favourite T-shirt, bought for me by John. And it had been one of the few things that still fitted me.

Friends came to visit bringing more flowers – nearly as many as after John's death. And letting their toddlers run around the house. A vase John had given me got smashed. I cowered in my room, hurting all over and feeling as if everything John and I had created was being destroyed.

I was quite careful, though, to get up and wash my tear-stained face before the health visitor arrived. But one morning she caught me out and gave me a stern lecture on the possibility of blood clots if I didn't keep moving around. After that I was more careful. I would get dressed in the mornings but then get back into bed and lie there listening out for unfamiliar cars in the street. It was something to do. I couldn't care less about blood clots. The realm of the dead seemed very much closer than the land of the living.

Looking back, I'm shocked really that my pathetic deceptions were enough to make anyone feel I was all right. Clearly I was in the most terrible state. Postnatal depression is so common and it doesn't take an enormous leap of the imagination to work out that someone giving birth to a posthumous baby might be more at risk.

Finally when the two weeks was up they all went away and left me alone. It took me until late afternoon on the first day to open a can of ravioli for mine and Ellie's lunch, but it felt like freedom, and at last I was on my own with my new little family to work out how we were going to survive.

Ellie was as good as her word and loved helping me care for her sister. She would fetch nappies and spend ages singing to Hope and dangling toys in front of her. Hope for her part was an exceptionally peaceable baby – not colicky as Ellie had been. Rarely crying, in fact, as if she knew we were a family treading on eggshells.

Although money was tight I kept Nanny Su on full-time during my maternity leave. In being granted maternity leave at all, which I wasn't entitled to at that point although the law has since changed, the deal was that I would go back after 20 weeks. I'd had two weeks off before the birth so Hope would be just over four months old when I went back to work, and in that time I had to recover mentally and physically. And so did Ellie.

Not for the first time, nor the last, did I reflect how lucky I was to be able to pay for what I needed because there was little or no other help on offer. I imagine if things had got so bad that I hadn't been able to care for the children, then Social Services would have stepped in. But how stupid to let things get that far.

Years later I found out about the work of the charity Home-Start UK. It was set up in 1973 by a visionary woman called Margaret Harrison. Her idea was that you don't have to wait until things get so bad that the State has to intervene – with all that entails. With a bit of back-up, parents can help other parents through tough times. It's natural, it's effective and very low cost. Volunteers, who must be parents themselves, undergo training (so they know how to help without interfering – very important!) and then are assigned to families in need. Had I known about Home-Start, or had anyone thought to mention it then, I think I would have taken help from a volunteer far more graciously than I took help from my family.

Typically, they work with families who are struggling because of illness, disability, addiction, or just plain bad luck, as well as bereavement. But you don't need to be in dire straits – as I was – to qualify for help. You simply have to have at least one child under five and be having trouble coping. The volunteer visits daily or weekly, as often as is needed, providing 'head space' for families to sort out the solutions to their own problems. They can give practical help such as taking the older children out for an afternoon and, if more specialist advice is needed, they can help sort out where to go for that, too. It's so successful that many parents who have been helped go on to train as volunteers themselves. Which just goes to prove – to my mind – that if you give a little bit of support at the right time you can not only avert disaster but you can actually allow someone who is vulnerable and down to grow into someone who is strong and able to help others.

In the year 2000 I became a trustee of Home-Start mainly because I was determined that no one who had been through anything like what I'd been through should be unaware of the fantastic service they provide. But in 1993 when I was alone and bereaved with a new baby and a four-year-old, no one thought I might need them nor did I know about them myself. Of course, I did have my family and my friends who were doing everything they could but — and this is so often overlooked — they were grieving, too . . . floundering around in a world that was as new to them as it was to me.

∞

At least I was still having counselling, once a week as soon as I was fit enough to leave the house. I took Hope with me to the sessions, settling her in her car seat at my feet while I blubbed away, still asking over and over again if I was going mad. Actually, by this time I think that I was.

While I freely admit I wouldn't be here now without the basic insights my counsellor was able to give me I am also convinced that she wasn't nearly qualified enough to help me properly. She had never counselled anyone who had had a posthumous baby before and nor had her supervisors. They did what they could but I was discovering more about it than they ever knew. Death is very like birth. Frighteningly similar, in fact. In birth a group of people labour away in a room until their number is swelled by one new person. In death, a similar thing happens and then one person in the room is no more. In those sleep-deprived, hormonally charged weeks after Hope was born I became very confused about the two processes. Someone arriving; someone leaving. Who was it? Who was alive and who was dead? I wasn't sure. I was parting company with reality.

Looking back I think I needed proper psychiatric advice. Certainly my grieving was prolonged by the lack of anyone really having any idea of what I was going through. There were aspects of John's death and Hope's birth that continued to haunt me for at least a decade afterwards, until I got the really in-depth help the situation demanded. Sitting in a church hall for an hour a week with a well-meaning volunteer who has been on a course is a bit like treating a severed limb with a Band-Aid and TCP. But that's all that was on offer.

Maybe everyone thought I was coping. Maybe they thought that the help I was getting was ample. Certainly my friends and family gave me all the support they knew how to give. If they didn't give any more it was because they didn't know how. Possibly the same was true of all the healthcare professionals I encountered. Maybe I did such a good job of covering up that I was the only person who realised just how precarious my mental state really was. Whatever the explanation, I eventually came to the conclusion in moments of lucidity that there was only one person who could safeguard my sanity – and that was me.

Having Nanny Su come in every day gave me a chance to rest and allowed me to spend time alone with Ellie. Whether it was that or whether it was just her naturally sweet nature, Ellie was never jealous of the baby. Even though I was braced for some my-Daddy's-gone-and-now-I-have-to-share-you-as-well tantrums, they never happened. And with Nanny Su at home with Hope I could drop Ellie at nursery, then spend a couple of hours simply being on my own. I would take the dog and I would walk miles until Rosie's legs all but dropped off. What was I thinking during those endless walks? I don't know. My memories of that time are largely blank and I stopped writing in my diary but I slept a lot – at least a couple of hours every afternoon to compensate for the broken nights. Rebuilding my strength mentally and physically.

At night, I had Hope in bed with me and I became adept at feeding her without really waking up. Naturally, Ellie slept with us as well. It was a big, six-feet-wide bed and there was easily room for all three of us. Medical opinion is divided on the advisability of sleeping with your baby but I don't see any other way you can cope if you are a single parent. I started out with a proper Moses basket by the side of the bed but after bringing Hope into bed with me for the first feed of the night – usually around 1am – I'd fall fast asleep again and still be out for the count by the time she finished feeding some half an hour later. So there was no chance I would wake up and put her back in the cot. The next time I would wake would be about 4am when she was ready for yet another feed.

∞

I struggled to give the children everything they would have had if John was alive. But it was a hopeless task. On our first Mother's Day alone, I wept for the fact that the year before John had forgotten all about it until the night before when he'd taken Ellie down to the park, hoisted her over the fence and asked her to pick – or rather steal – a bunch of daffodils for me. How was I to top that? I took both girls to Hampstead Heath for a picnic – Hope in the buggy; Ellie walking alongside and the dog on a lead. There was an icy wind blowing and both girls were grizzling. Nonetheless I sat Ellie down on a bench, tied the dog lead to the buggy and started to unpack the food. Another dog went past, Rosie lunged after it and the buggy started to topple. I whirled round to grab the buggy and stop it tipping over but as I did so I caught Ellie on the face with the hard plastic sandwich box. She was bleeding and crying. Hope started crying. And so did I. It was misery and Ellie bore a tiny scar on the side of her nose for the rest of her life – a reminder of our first Mothering Sunday without John.

The fact was that I was barely coping. And my friends, loyal and supportive as they were, had their own lives to get on with. Their own small children to raise. Although they did what they could for me – and more. At Easter when Hope was two months old, Alastair and Fiona once more gathered us up and took us off on holiday in Mallorca with a bunch of their friends who – yet again – I didn't know. And again – as I had been in France – I was amazed at the tolerance of people who were having their holidays wrecked by a weepy widow and her two little children. Even in my slightly loopy state I was conscious of the fact that, desperate though my situation was, it allowed me to see sides of people that I might otherwise never have known about.

One member of our party was the politician Peter Mandelson who even at that stage had earned the soubriquet in the press of the Prince of Darkness. John had known him and I'd met him briefly beforehand but nothing about his urbane, slightly cynical exterior prepared me for the astonishing kindness he showed me. Not only did he drive us to and from the beach every day in his hire car, then out to dinner in the evening, but he was adept at collapsing and opening out the large and unwieldy baby buggy, fitting the car seat, and had no embarrassment whatsoever about walking into a bar with a nappy bag slung over his shoulder. Even better, as an early riser he didn't mind looking after all the children in the morning, allowing the parents to sleep on. Ellie would slide out of bed when she woke up to go and bang on the future European Commissioner's door while I stayed in bed giving Hope her morning feed.

∞

In June, I returned to work. I'd planned to get Hope onto a bottle by the time I went back but my peaceable, easy-going baby certainly knew how to dig her heels in when she wanted. Babycare books will tell you that no child will starve itself and they'll give in eventually. Clearly

Hope hadn't read the books! Or maybe it was just that my resolve was weaker than Hope's. She adamantly refused any nourishment while I was out of the house from 9am to 7pm, and Nanny Su with her childcare certificates and 10 years' experience could not get her to take a bottle. So for the first six weeks that I was back at work I would drive home in the middle of the day – from the South Bank to Crouch End – sit and breastfeed for 20 minutes while wolfing down a cheese sandwich then jump in the car and drive back to the office. It was exhausting and I was exhausted.

Luckily, by the time she was six months old Hope could sit up and drink from a feeder cup, which she did quite happily, allowing me to spend the full day at work. But she continued to feed from me at night, taking most of her nourishment then. My breasts were so over-stimulated through providing so much milk at night that they leaked copiously all day, threatening to stain my work clothes. At least every couple of hours I would have to creep into the cupboard where we stored the clothes for fashion shoots and, with the help of a hand-held breast pump, express what seemed like pints of milk into baby bottles. Rather than throw it away I would store it in a cooler bag with ice-packs so I could freeze it when I got home – in the vain belief that one day Hope would take it from a bottle. And more than one chic fashionista whom I bumped into in the corridors of IPC asked me why it was I never seemed to go anywhere without a cooler bag.

My employers were as kind as they knew how to be and more generous than most. At least I had the fashion cupboard to sit in. Many women I know have had to express milk in the toilets at their work. But had I been able to return part-time for those first weeks both Hope and I would have been a great deal more comfortable.

When my life started to look up – nearly a decade later – I began campaigning through the pages of the maga-

zines I worked on for more flexibility for women returning to work after having babies. Eventually it won me a
Lifetime Achievement award from the Work/Life Balance
Trust. But in 1993 all I got was mastitis. This is an infection in the breast caused when one of the ducts gets
blocked – often as a result of not being able to breastfeed
as regularly as necessary. I woke up one night – alone in
the house except for the children – with one breast hard,
swollen and very painful to the touch. I was hot and feverish but managed to crawl out of bed and find the
thermometer. I had a temperature of 104 degrees. One of
the scariest things about being a single parent is being
ill. I rang for the doctor, took some paracetamol to bring
my temperature down and set about applying alternately
hot and cold compresses until he arrived and gave me a
prescription which Nanny Su could get made up in the
morning. Antibiotics soon cleared up the infection but I
was tortured by what would happen if I lost consciousness for any reason – or couldn't get to the phone. I taught
Ellie, still only four years old, to dial 999.

It was equally bad when one or other of the children
got ill. They only ever had minor ailments but with a
sick child I would be stuck in the house, dependent on
someone else to bring the essentials of milk, newspapers
and Calpol. One night Ellie had an ear infection and was
up crying most of the night. She finally dropped off to
sleep at 6am, at which point Hope woke up wanting her
breakfast.

On days like these I still went in to work. Not just
because there was no concept of family leave in those days
but also because work was far more restful than home.
After all, at work I could make a cup of coffee without
worrying about a child knocking it over and scalding
herself. I even got to eat my lunch in peace. Work
colleagues rarely spit baby rice out at you.

In campaigning for greater work/life balance, I have always emphasised that it is balance that's needed. I have never been anti-work; nor anti-mothers who stay at home. Being alone trapped in a house with tiny children is not a soft option. Some women can manage but I most certainly could not. When John was alive and I was at home with Ellie, admittedly doing some freelance work, I could just about endure it. Even so I'd wait like a dog for the sound of his key in the lock and some adult stimulation. But after his death, the idea of being home alone with my grief, my memories, two very young children and no one coming home at night – no respite whatsoever – was unendurable.

I was lucky in that I had a job that was interesting. But it wasn't just that. I loved my job and it loved me back. Despite my tiredness and the fact that after paying for childcare I was really no better off than if I'd stayed at home on benefits, I found work even more satisfying than I ever had in the halcyon days when I only had myself to think about. Things that I would have found difficult in the past became simply stuff that had to be got through.

If there was a pile of urgent paperwork on my desk, I would just close my mind to all distractions and plough through it until it was done. Telling a writer that their copy needed to be totally rewritten, or a photographer that a shoot had to be redone, held few fears for me after everything I'd been through. In the office I was clear, calm and objective. I could pass on the unwelcome news in a dispassionate and objective way with none of the blustering and evasions that so irritate freelance contributors.

Office politics left me unperturbed. Sure it was irritating if someone undermined me or passed off my ideas as their own. But I'd survived worse, far worse. Just like in the film *Unbreakable* where Bruce Willis survives a train crash and believes he can then never be killed – so I'd survived something so awful that nothing that happened in an office could ever scare me again.

And I discovered a great truth about what really works at work – and that's to coin the Nike slogan: Just Do It. Time and time again I would see people get in a great state about something they'd been asked to do or a situation that seemed unfathomable. It seemed they would rather obsess about it than actually have a go at it. In previous jobs I'd been the same. I'd made myself thoroughly miserable by fussing and fretting so much that sometimes I fussed and fretted myself right out of the job.

Now I knew that there was almost nothing that couldn't be resolved by simply focusing intently on what it was that needed to be done and ignoring all distractions. My career flourished and prospered. At that time, *Woman* magazine was riding high on an unprecedented wave of success, overtaking its IPC stablemate *Woman's Own* for the first time ever. And I was a senior and valued part of the crack team producing it. Every six months the audited figures for our circulation were published and each time we were up again on the previous set. We'd have a party, drink some champagne and then get back down to work.

Home life, however, was much more problematic. I was lucky in that I didn't need to be at work until 10am, giving me time to get the girls up and dressed and sort myself out as well. I developed a 'work uniform' that always included a jacket over the top of a skirt or dress. This was to hide the inevitable baby sick on my shoulder. There was even time for me to walk Ellie round to nursery, giving us special time alone together. In fact, over the years, I have always been lucky enough to be able to walk the children to school before heading off to work. It has given me a chance to meet other mums and stay involved in school activities.

The downside though was that I couldn't leave work early. On weeknights I would rush to get home from work at around 7pm – if I was lucky – which would give me two hours to spend with the girls. I decided on a 9pm bedtime for them both, otherwise I'd never see them in the evening. I'd play with them, bath them, read to them and put them to bed. Then I'd go back downstairs to do some housework and fix myself something to eat.

After my early experiences of running out of essentials, I became meticulously organised. Later on in my career I'd incorporate those strategies into the advice pages of the magazines I edited, boosting sales and earning me a reputation as some sort of domestic diva. But back in the early days of single parenthood it was simply survival. Milk and newspapers were delivered every day and on Fridays I would do the big supermarket shop, working strictly to a list and a menu planner. There was always food in the house for Nanny Su to cook for the children but often I was too tired even to heat something up for myself. One night I wrote in my diary, 'Tired, so tired, don't know when I'll ever not feel tired again. Had a lump of cheese and a walnut whip for supper – at least there's fibre in the walnut, I suppose.'

If weeknights were bad then the weekends were worse. Other friends as well as Terry would invite me over for supper and lunch (I later found out they would call each other up so there was a bit of a rota going) but even this left acres of time when I was utterly alone with the children.

There is so much that's ghastly about being a single parent. Just one aspect is having no grown-up to share things with. I ate supper – such as it was – alone every night, with no one to discuss what to watch on TV. I woke up in the morning without anyone to review the day with or make plans with or to read the Sunday papers with.

I soon discovered that it was easy to slide into a pit of hopelessness and sluttish behaviour. Who was there to see if we didn't eat at the table? Or didn't get dressed at weekends. Or comb our hair? And who – after all – could judge me anyway given all we had been through? But after a few Saturdays when we stayed in our pyjamas all day and ate baked beans out of the can, I realised it was making me feel worse not better. And that when the invitation came to go and see friends, it was harder than ever to get our act together and look presentable if we had to start from such a low base.

So with heavy heart – because I was always tired and I wanted someone to just come in and look after me – I resolved that on Saturdays and Sundays I would get showered and dressed as soon as I woke up (once the girls were up and about it became impossible), just as I did on weekdays. And we would sit up and eat at the table. And I would cook vegetables and fresh food instead of having stuff out of tins. And most important of all, I kept a bag packed with Hope's change stuff plus drinks for the girls and a couple of books for Ellie permanently hanging over the banister in the hall. If we wanted to go out I could just pick up the bag and run, rather than scrabbling around looking for all the things we needed, by which time Hope would need changing, or I'd have to give the girls some lunch and the moment would pass.

∞

As August approached so did the first anniversary of John's death. In my naivety I thought this – while sad – would basically be a good day. A whole year survived and the comfort of knowing that the next year could only be easier. I could not have been more wrong.

For a start it wasn't just the one day. Right from the beginning of the month I began to feel very odd. Everything was so like the year before – yet so unlike. The weather was very similar. And needless to say friends and family were departing on holiday. It was as if we were all re-enacting the events of August 1992 but with one ghastly difference – John had been wiped from the picture. Each day that passed I had almost exact recall of what had happened that day a year ago. I remembered what John had said. How he'd hinted that he might not last much longer, then refused to speak about it. I remembered his good days and his bad days, and how he'd taken me and Ellie to the ballet for my birthday. It was as if I was being forced to plod through it all again, to relive the times I'd got it wrong, all the moments when I could have helped but didn't – but without any prospect of ever putting it right. Even my movements became slower and my thinking got woolly. My dreams that he was still alive – always vivid – became overpowering until I would wake sweating and confused in the morning not knowing what was conscious and what was subconscious.

The sixteenth of August, the day before the anniversary, was the worst. The very pit of despair as I spent the whole day in flashbacks reliving his last agonies and the hopeless dash to the hospital.

When the day itself dawned it was almost a relief. John had died early in the morning. Surely the flashbacks would stop: I'd relived the whole thing. Terry took me to place flowers on the grave in the morning, then in to work. It never occurred to me to take the day off. I craved distraction. During the morning I discovered that a sub-editor had made a mess of a feature I'd commissioned. I walked over to her desk to point out where she had gone wrong and she looked at me in such a dozy way that suddenly I found myself screaming at her. There was a rushing noise in my head and in my eyes and I couldn't stop myself. How could she be so incompetent and still be alive when John was dead? Several colleagues rushed up and pulled me away. They took me into the editor's office where I dissolved in tears. David then took me out for a long lunch and plied me with wine and a salade niçoise – which I couldn't eat – and, probably in desperation, told me the story of his life while I sat stunned by the raging fury in my head.

Over the years I was to discover the terrible truth that anniversaries are always awful. An awfulness made worse by the expectations of other people. I remember on the fifth anniversary of Princess Diana's death there were all these stories in the papers about how her young sons would be over the worst of it now. Now I don't know them – obviously – but how could anyone seriously think that to have lived five years without their mother was better than only to have lived one or two? It's insane. But then the way other people behave often is. Something I've forced myself to become very disciplined about is visiting the graves one or two days before the actual anniversary. This was after a colleague remarked sniffily that she was surprised not to see fresh flowers there when she had dropped by. I'd brought them, of course, but arrived later in the day than her. As chief mourner you are appointed keeper of the flame and other people feel badly if you don't behave in a way they think is fitting.

Surviving anniversaries is really just a question of battening down the hatches and trying to keep out of harm's way. Above all don't schedule any tricky meetings. A bereaved mother once asked me – after she'd bawled out a client on an anniversary, who promptly took his business elsewhere – whether anniversaries ever got any better. I had to tell her no, they don't. But you do get better at predicting what's going to happen and getting through the day without incident. There is no avoiding it altogether, though. Even if you had no calendar and didn't know the date, it's still as if there's a clock inside your head counting down to the anniversary. The only progress I've found is that the build-up does become less with time. That first year, the anniversary actually took me around six weeks to get through. Now it's down to a day or two either side – and for me the day before is always the worst. On the day before the twelfth anniversary of John's death, I scraped the side of my car while parking it in a bay that I use every single day. My lovely car! I got out, inspected the damage and wept. Then I remembered the date and cursed John for haunting me like this. But it also gave me a secure feeling. The biggest fear that anyone has when someone they love dies is that they will forget. You don't. No matter how much time has passed it's still a good idea to take public transport.

Chapter Five

∞

WHAT WOULD JOHN
HAVE THOUGHT?

Nobody wants to hear this but the truth is that the second year of mourning is much worse than the first. The first year is awful; you are learning to live alone, going through all those things that have to be got through: Christmas, Valentine's Day, Mother's Day, birthdays and the anniversary. And then the second year comes and nothing is any better. You are still alone, only now there isn't even the novelty of it all to get you through. Your only reward for being so good and strong and brave during the first awful year is . . . more of the same. For ever. As far as the rest of the world is concerned you are recovering and they have their own lives to get on with but in fact you feel far worse than you ever did before.

As the second Christmas without John loomed I began to panic at the thought. Right from when I was a child up until John's death, I'd always loved Christmas. But then I discovered it can be the most frightening and hateful time of year if you are on your own. I remember driving to work at the beginning of December trying to listen to the radio and realising it would be a non-stop diet of festive tunes for the next three weeks. Every magazine I opened (including my own) and every newspaper was full of heart-warming stories stressing the importance of togetherness at this time of year. I felt like a reject from life. The only person not worthy of having a complete family at Christmas.

Earlier in the year my oldest schoolfriend Christina had moved to Japan with her husband and two little boys. She had written to me suggesting I come out and stay with them. It seemed like an insane idea. Who would travel half way around the world with two young children just to get away from 'I Wish It Could Be Christmas Every Day' on the radio? But the idea took shape in my mind. I couldn't really afford it. After paying for our living expenses and childcare there was little money left over for luxuries like travel. But the magazine was doing so well that I was beginning to earn bonuses for the first time in my life. I'd just received one which would cover the airfare for me plus a child's fare for Ellie. As a baby Hope would travel free sitting on my lap. Christina generously promised to bankroll us when we got there. We just had to get there.

After the hell of Christmas shopping right up to the line the year before I'd been much more efficient this time around. I may have felt worse than ever but in purely practical terms I was definitely doing better. Only months before I'd found it hard to get out of the door with baby and child without forgetting the nappy bag or still wearing my slippers. Now I simply booked the flights – another advance on the previous year – quickly distributed the gifts I'd already bought, promising everyone else Japanese artefacts on my return, and made lists of what we needed to take. Lists, I'd discovered, were the key to sanity.

There was no way I could pack the night before – hastily stuffing a suitcase as I had always done in my old life. I set aside the Saturday evening a full week before our departure and worked from a detailed list filling the two big cheap soft-sided bags I'd bought in Brent Cross. Suitcases were out of the question – far too unwieldy. I estimated that I could carry one bag on each shoulder and push Hope in the buggy while Ellie walked alongside. She was a well-behaved child and I hoped I could trust her to hang on to the handle of the buggy in the crowds and confusion of the airport.

∞

There was a difficult moment when I went through passport control. My passport is in my maiden name of Nicholson but the children's passports obviously had the name Merritt. 'Does their father know you are taking them out of the country?' the passport official asked. 'I shouldn't think so, he's dead,' I snapped. It struck me afterwards that I didn't need to be so nasty but what earthly use was it asking such a question? If I really had been kidnapping the children, would I have owned up to it?

The flight was 16 hours. Ellie made herself a little nest with a blanket and pillow and slept the whole way. Hope jumped up and down on my stomach non-stop. It was a Virgin flight and the cabin crew were delightful. Once the meals were served and the lights dimmed they took it in turns to look after Hope while I got some sleep. This was fantastic – far easier than being at home. Maybe the answer for exhausted single parents is to spend as much time as possible on planes. At Narita airport Virgin arranged for me to be collected in one of those airport buggies, bypassing customs and delivering us straight to where Christina was waiting with her car.

Her husband was working for a telecoms company in Tokyo and the family, including Lawrence then four and William aged two, were living in a large airy flat in the nightclub district of Roppongi. Before she had children Christina had worked in the City and on Wall Street, and she is easily the most organised person on the planet. She had got everything ready for us, right down to nappies and baby wipes laid out on a change mat in the spare room. I collapsed into their warm, hospitable family home and abandoned myself to being looked after. It was bliss.

Christina had brought an artificial Christmas tree with

her from England and imported a frozen turkey from America. I'd packed a Christmas pudding in my luggage, so on Christmas Day we had a properly traditional lunch with all the trimmings. She even found a single ludicrously expensive log – very hard to come by in Tokyo – so we could have an open fire in the fireplace, which incredibly did work and didn't fill the flat with smoke as we had feared. I was glad for the children's sake that there was a truly festive atmosphere – I didn't want to bring them up with bad memories of Christmas – but for myself I found it overwhelming. After we'd eaten I left the children playing and went out for a walk.

It was a blessed release to be able to step outside the Christmassy flat into the cool, fresh sharp air of a city where it was just another day. The shops were open. Preparations were underway for the New Year, which is a far bigger celebration in Japan. I walked about for a couple of hours, looking in shops and inhaling the scent of the pine fronds that are everywhere at that time of year, and resolved that whatever happened I wanted to be as far away from home as I could for Christmas in future. At last, I could understand why John's family had travelled so ceaselessly after his mother's death.

I spent two weeks in Tokyo with Christina. We went sightseeing, visiting temples and Shinto shrines and even went to see some kabuki theatre, which we both adored. Christina had a Filipina maid to help her with the children who would babysit if we needed, but most of the time we dragged all the kids along with us. Pre-recession, Japan was still fantastically expensive for Western visitors so tourists were not a common sight. Two tall frizzy-haired gaijin with a gaggle of tots led to quite a few surreptitious glances and even disgusted snorts. We didn't care. We were high on the experience of discovering such a new and different culture. We travelled everywhere by public transport, carting the two buggies up and down endless flights of stairs while keeping tight hold of Ellie and Lawrence. We lost our way often and once also lost Hope's favourite teddy during the rush hour at Ginza underground station. This station is famously so crowded that commuters are pushed onto the trains with long poles but Hope was bawling her head off so I had no choice but to plunge back into the crowds looking for Ted – emerging triumphant, holding him above my head as the crowds swirled me back through the barrier to where Christina was waiting with all the children.

In the evenings we read up all we could about the country where Christina was making her home. We learned to use chopsticks and taught the children to do so as well, even though they usually preferred to shovel up rice with the serving spoons. We tried to make them understand about wiping their hands with hot towels before eating in restaurants and not let them get away with their favourite trick of putting them on their heads. Some of the customs and etiquette passed us by, however. Like nose blowing, for instance.

Blowing your nose in public is frowned on in Japan. It is even preferable to wear a surgical mask and let your nose run behind it rather than give one discreet blow and wipe. In the cold winter air all the children soon had streaming noses. Running out of tissues I took to stowing toilet rolls in the pocket of my raincoat to wipe noses. Once we entered a restaurant and the warmth after the cold outside set them all off. I toured our table wiping away four lots of snot until Christina realised that fellow diners around us were gagging and leaving their tables. We later discovered that it couldn't have been more disgusting to local sensibilities if I'd been wiping the children's bottoms.

But the sheer differentness of Japan energised me. I returned home and to the office feeling more positive than I had done in ages. To find that not everyone was impressed that I was finding my feet again. 'Oh, hark at Superwoman,' snapped one colleague as I was describing my adventures. My first realisation that some people are definitely more comfortable when you are not coping.

∞

Even though I didn't know it at the time, and in fact was feeling so much worse, the truth was that I *was* coping. Gradually, piece by piece, I was putting together a new life for myself and the children. The weekdays were devoted to work and getting Ellie to school (where she was always known as Eleanor). I still did all the house-work at night after the children had gone to bed and did the supermarket shop on the way home from work on Friday nights, to leave the weekends free for my girls. But without much money and no other adult for company the weekends were often barren wastelands. We spent a lot of time at the park and when it got too cold for that I scraped together the money to join a health club.

Most Saturday and Sunday afternoons I would drive the girls over to Finchley and we would go swimming together. At this stage Ellie was five and Hope was only one so it wasn't really swimming. I would sit in the baby pool with them while they splashed around in their arm bands. Or take Hope on my hip into the big pool while I helped Ellie learn to swim. I longed to swim myself. I wasn't getting any exercise at all and craved to move my muscles in a way that wasn't about carrying children or shopping.

There was actually a crèche at the health club, which was one of the reasons why I had chosen it, but it was for very little children. Ellie at five was too old and Hope wouldn't go to it without her. I began to realise the essen-tial truth about crèches. By the time your child will stay in one happily, they are too old to need it. Luckily both girls were fearless in water and once Ellie had learned to do doggy paddle we could do slow lengths of the pool together, Ellie swimming alongside me and Hope riding on my back. We must have swum miles that way.

Driving to the health club, changing, swimming, then ordering a plate of pasta to eat in the cafeteria took at least four hours. Sometimes, I would manage to tack on a visit to the cinema on the way home afterwards, but more often than not such sophistication and forward planning was beyond us and I would then forget something like the times of the movies, or omit to put the swimming stuff in the car. One weekend I got it hopelessly wrong (leaving the house was even more pandemonium than usual) and not only forgot the swimming things but failed to check whether there was anything suitable for children showing at the multiplex. There wasn't, and while both children cried about being deprived of both swimming and a movie, I sat in the car park and cried, too, about always, always having to do everything on my own.

∞

More than 18 months had passed since John's death and I was still dreaming about him most nights – usually that he wasn't dead and that he'd come back to me. Occasionally I even had an orgasm in my sleep. But when I woke I ached for the touch of a real live man. An aching which, to my shame at the time, had begun only months after John's death. I'd managed to suppress the feelings while I was pregnant and then breastfeeding. Although once I had noted in my diary: 'Went to the hairdresser today. As he washed my hair in the backwash I started to tingle all over. It has been so-o-o-o long since a man touched me!'

How long should you wait after a partner dies before beginning another relationship? It has always struck me as odd that neither the Church nor the State would have any choice but to sanction a remarriage that came even just days after a death. The legal position is very clearly 'till death us do part'. And once the death has occurred then the relationship ceases to exist. Finito. End of story.

The moral position, however, lags a long way behind the legal. There is very definitely a taste factor about starting a sexual relationship too soon, although the same people who are so quick to condemn would presumably have much less of a problem – if they had a problem at all – with someone who was newly divorced, or even just separated, doing so.

Sexual desires do not get buried in the ground along with the coffin, yet we do expect the widowed to get through the first few grim and lonely months without any sexual comfort. It's a case of double-thinking that must cause a great deal of pain – although I suspect the widowers are cut more slack.

I have never found any definitive writing on the subject but a quick and totally unscientific straw poll revealed that, in terms of taste, the people I questioned feel a widow should wait at least a year before starting a new relationship, maybe more. A widower is allowed to do what-a-man's-gotta-do after about three months. That's the thing about grief. It is utterly unreconstructed. It throws people back on their deepest, most atavistic emotions and widows are most definitely required to act with more decorum than men in the same position.

For me, being pregnant – and then breastfeeding – meant that sex (however much I missed it) seemed to be totally out of the question. No one would be attracted to me anyway, I reasoned, and the longings I had could be kept private and not acted upon. Once Hope was weaned, though, I did rather want to meet someone. My love for John was undiminished but . . . but . . . but . . . I was still only 37, for God's sake. I wasn't dead. I wanted to love and be loved by someone who was living. I even believed it might be possible for me to have more children if the right person came along. I really did think it could be that simple.

When I was a young woman I hadn't ever thought about dating as such. With the supreme confidence of youth I had assumed that if you met someone and liked them, then they probably liked you and you'd spend some time hanging out together. There were no games. No hesitation. No fear of commitment. The *durm und strang* of does he like me/will he phone me had more or less passed me by. Starting a relationship was like falling off a log. And ending one was no big deal either. So you didn't get on? Plenty more fish in the sea! I was never even quite sure about what happened to those three men pursuing me around Blackpool at the National Union of Students conference. At the age of 22 I had fallen deeply in love with John. And that was that for the rest of my life. Or so I had thought.

The first object of my post-widowhood affections was someone John had worked with occasionally. He was tall, lanky and in a dim, very dim, light looked rather like John. He took me out for lunch one day – as many of John's other colleagues had done. I'd finally shed the last half-stone of the baby weight and I was wearing a new black suit and looking, I thought, very slinky. We went to my usual haunt – Joe Allen's in Covent Garden – and drank a little too much. It was fun. We started out talking about John but then we talked about other stuff, too. When he kissed me goodbye – on the cheek – I was sure he lingered longer than someone who was just a friend might have done.

I waited a few days, then rang and invited him to dinner. A dinner party I hastily assembled once he'd said yes. No couples to make things obvious, just a bunch of friends. He came and appeared to enjoy himself. He was the last to leave and this time the goodnight kiss definitely was lingering. I was ecstatic. I rang him again. He rang me. We talked for hours on the phone. He came over for a drink one evening after the children had gone to bed (I could never get a babysitter) and we kissed and talked and drank some more. He didn't leave until 1am. I expected him to call the next day but . . . nothing!

I waited one, two, three days, then I rang and got the answerphone. I rang again. Still the answerphone. I left messages. One a day. Then several in one day. Then the answerphone didn't pick up and the phone just rang out. This had never happened before in my life. I had completely missed the bit where someone lets you know they don't want to see you by not returning your calls. I assumed there must be something wrong with his phone. I rang British Telecom and got the line checked. It was working fine. After about 10 days of this I became completely hysterical. I rang over and over again. If I got the answerphone I sobbed into it uncontrollably. Eventually he called back.

'We have to meet,' he said and named a bar. Of course, as usual I didn't have anyone to babysit but he was adamant we had to meet that night in a bar, in public – not at home. I still didn't know what was going on. I called a friend who lived miles away and didn't even have children of her own and begged a favour – this was important to me. Then I dressed with particular care and set off, thinking all this confusion about phones would be resolved, we'd have a lovely evening and everything was going to be okay.

He was waiting for me when I arrived. And came straight to the point. 'You're scaring me,' he said. And then he told me he was leaving for Bosnia in the morning. Even in my crazed state the irony of the situation didn't escape me. Clearly a war zone was less frightening than my company!

I was utterly, utterly crushed. Foolishly I'd been dreaming that I was going to get some sort of life back. Only to have it snatched away from me. I didn't know then that this is just the sort of stuff that happens in the brutal world of dating. That people, even quite nice people, do come on strong and then have second thoughts and back away. This had never happened to me before. I was devastated, torn apart and burning with shame. I thought I must be irredeemably vile to make someone behave this way. The pain was like a knife in my heart. Ridiculous as it sounds there were days when I could hardly bear to go on. I would drag myself out of bed in the morning, crawl into work and simply go through the motions. At night, once the children had gone to bed, I would crawl back into bed myself and cry until I was overwhelmed with sleep.

And I was racked with guilt about feeling this way; desperately ashamed of the fact that I was suffering such extremes of emotion over someone who, to be frank, I hardly knew, when the man I truly loved, the father of my children, was dead. My counsellor was way out of her depth and unable to help me – reduced to saying over and over again that it would be a good idea to get to know someone before becoming involved with them. Well, obviously! But I couldn't help myself. My feelings were rioting out of control.

There was no one who could help me and explain to me what I later worked out, that I was feeling the pain of John's death all over again, as if for the first time. And that I would continue to relive that loss every time with every other loss I suffered, however minor, until it had worked through my system. All I knew was that the pain was unbearable and I would never, never allow myself to be so vulnerable ever again. The carefree, confident young girl had gone forever. I should have been crying for her. But I didn't know that.

Nor did my friends. There was a phase when they all seemed to be organising dinner parties with the express purpose of introducing me to the one man they knew who wasn't already fixed up. It was kind of them to try but these were always disasters. I don't know if it's the same for everyone, but the thought of *having* to get on with someone makes me take an instant dislike to them. A bit like books. If someone assures me I'll love a particular book then I know I'll hate it. I have a childish need to discover things for myself.

∞

Many, many months later, and after the second anniversary had passed, I did meet someone else. In fact, it was someone I'd known for years. He lived and worked in the North of England making only occasional visits to London on business, when we would get together. I liked him a lot. He cheered me up and made me laugh but my heart had closed over and calcified. I wasn't going to risk feeling anything for anyone ever again. I refused to refer to him as my boyfriend or describe what we had as a 'relationship'. I never allowed him to stay the night nor get to know the children. Weeks would pass with me dodging his phone calls. Sometimes when he had made a special trip to London I would cancel our date at the last minute. I was behaving, in fact, in exactly the way that had caused me so much pain. Worse really, because it went on for longer.

Bill, as I'll call him, to protect his privacy, was good-looking, funny and kind. A bit bumptious and over-bearing, which in a rare moment of self-knowledge he informed me was just as well as it allowed him to force his way past my defences. If I would open up more, he told me, I could attract a more sensitive man.

He may as well have been speaking in tongues for all

I understood. But I saw him just often enough to stave off the pangs of loneliness. Work and the children continued to be my main sources of comfort.

∞

As I got my routines sorted out I was able to take more pleasure in being a parent. Even if I was having to do it on my own. Ellie was a quiet child, startlingly beautiful, with deep auburn curls, a heart-shaped face and heavy-lidded blue eyes that were so big they never closed properly even when she was asleep. She loved ballet, ponies, wearing party dresses and the colour pink. She read avidly and wrote endless stories, turning some into home-made books, which she also illustrated. She invented a school for orphaned princesses where they learned ballet and to ride ponies, usually while wearing a lot of pink. Her favourite character was usually called Rose. This was all a bit tame for Hope, who preferred more action, so Ellie invented another character for her – a rabbit called Hope-Bunny – who got into all sorts of naughty scrapes. At night they would lie in bed together and Ellie would relate the further adventures of Hope-Bunny.

Hope had grown from being a peaceable baby into a cheerily independent toddler with tufty red hair and piercing green eyes, as opposed to her sister's dreamy blue. She still didn't cry much but made what we called 'baby dinosaur noises' if the bigger children's rough games got too much and she needed rescuing. She was quite a quirky child and went through various odd phases. The weirdest – which lasted several weeks – was when she believed she was a cat and insisted on eating her food out of a bowl on the floor. I discovered one of the liberations of raising children on your own is that you don't have to sweat the small stuff. Hope wanted to eat off the floor?

Fine! It didn't bother me in the least. Eventually she returned to eating at the table of her own accord. I would see other couples with young children wind each other up into terrible states about potty-training and reading ages, and all manner of developmental milestones. Yet our home-life was terribly, terribly calm. I didn't shout at the children, however tired I was. They didn't squabble with each other. We were alive. We were together. We were grateful for that.

Indeed we were coping pretty well but I was conscious that the girls needed proper male role models in their life. My brothers were fantastic. Not only did Jeremy continue drilling me in good financial management, but Hugh regularly drove up to London after finishing work in Essex and installed security lights, window locks, put up shelves. He even supervised a new roof being put on the house when the leaks from the old one got too bad. Both went out of their way to spend time with the girls – doing things I would never do with them like flinging them up in the air and dangling them upside down by their feet. Jeremy even drove Ellie around a field on the back of his new pride and joy, a Honda Fireblade motorbike, her red-gold hair streaming in the wind and a huge beam on her face.

Alastair also made sure to spend as much time as possible with the girls. My social life, such as it was at the time, revolved around taking the kids to weekend lunches or suppers at friends' houses. Ali never cared much for the adult conversation at these gatherings, preferring to organise a game of football outside with all the children – his, mine and everyone else's – or if it was raining simply read to them while the rest of the adults got on with their chatting and gossiping. As a non-drinker he would always volunteer to be the driver and usually drove me and the children home – along with his mother-in-law Audrey and anyone else who needed a lift – which meant that I got to slurp down a glass of wine or two. I was very disciplined about never drinking on my own, which meant I hardly drank. But I felt so deprived of adult pleasures that I started smoking quite heavily – although never in front of the children. I managed to justify it to myself by saying that it wasn't smoking that deprived me of a husband and why the hell shouldn't I have a treat?

Occasionally Alastair would call in on his way home from work, too, just to check we were all okay, fulfilling the promise he had made to John always to look after us. When he later became famous, much was made in the press of the fact that many women found him wildy attractive. He has certainly become a good-looking man but to be honest, to me, he has looked the same way since I met him. And I regard him as my third brother. One night he dropped by with the news that he was thinking of changing jobs. At that time he was political editor of *Today* but while on holiday the then leader of the opposition, Tony Blair, had detoured to where the Campbells were staying in France and asked Ali to become his press secretary. Did I think he should do it? Did I think John would have thought he should do it? I actually thought it was a bit of a step down. It certainly was in salary terms but also, to me at that time – as it certainly had been to John – journalism was not just a job: it was a calling. To become effectively a PR seemed to be the sort of thing you did if you could no longer hack it.

John had been conspicuously apolitical. He worked from the assumption that anyone in power was up to no good and his sole concerns were to expose wrongdoing and protect the underdog. I was more conventionally left wing but I believed, like John, that journalists were better off owing no political allegiance. Although in truth, it was also that neither of us was very keen on signing up to any sort of organisation. Unlike Alastair we were not in the least tribal, both being naturally observers rather than supporters.

Fiona was the most political of the four of us. Her parents were lifelong Labour party members and she and her brother Gavin grew up steeped in political discourse. When Alastair got together with Fiona her passion for social justice was one of the things that attracted him to her and after his breakdown he too became much more involved in politics and the Labour party.

I could see that Alastair was keen to help Tony and with the Conservatives having been in power for 15 years at that point anything that could help a Labour Government get elected was worth doing. I assumed he would do the job for a bit and then go back into newspapers after the election. His instincts and grasp of tabloid journalism made me believe his true destiny was to be editor of the *Daily Mirror*. I still hope it happens.

We sat discussing it in my kitchen. In the end I decided (not that I could possibly have known) that John would have thought that to be that close to power was an unmissable opportunity, even if it did mean being a poacher turned gamekeeper. So I told him: 'Do it – but take notes.' And he did.

∞

But Alastair wasn't the only one moving on. In the spring of 1995, when Hope was two and Ellie six. I received a phone call at work that was to change my life. Was I interested in editing the women's magazine *Prima* – then the biggest-selling monthly magazine in Britain? You bet I was! *Prima* was then still owned by the company that refused me promotion when I was pregnant with Ellie and who had turned me down for a job when they found out John was ill. Possibly not the greatest of employers for someone bringing up two young children on her own but

I didn't care. An editorship was still an editorship and this was one of the big ones.

Despite being head-hunted I still had to go through several gruelling interviews, presenting my ideas for the magazine. Eventually, I was told there was just one more hurdle. I had to fly to Paris for an interview with Axel Ganz, the International President of Gruner + Jahr. He had a very busy diary and the date for my trip was finally fixed – for his convenience and at very short notice. I managed to book a day's holiday from *Woman* on some spurious pretext, but came home to find my then nanny in tears. She had recently discovered she was pregnant – an unplanned pregnancy – and was finding looking after two small children exhausting. She had been signed off on a week's sick leave by her doctor.

Great! Not only could I not get to work without a nanny but I couldn't get to the interview that would give me a better paid job so I could afford more childcare. Because I was at work all the time I was not part of the local mums' network. I had no back-up. There was no one I could automatically turn to. I rang everyone I could think of, and eventually my cousin Sue stepped into the breach. The next day I flew off to Paris wearing my one good suit and carrying a borrowed briefcase – I didn't have one of my own – containing my presentation.

The interview turned out to be no more than a formality. Axel was charming – German by birth but living in France and fluent in English. He is a former magazine editor who became a multi-millionaire businessman by launching a string of successful magazines. He disdained publishers who chased the advertising pound at the expense of integrity or who indulged in circulation-building gimmicks. A magazine should sell on the quality of its editorial alone, he would say. And his did. *Prima* in France sold well over a million. *Femme Actuelle*, the weekly he created, sold over two million. Even his travel magazine *Geo* was selling half a million. The man was a publishing genius and he was about to give me my big break. He was and still is my magazine hero and, no matter what the difficulties, I planned to absorb every last thing he could teach me.

My first day as editor was 12 July 1995, and I had already hired as my deputy Lucy Bulmer, who was features editor of *Woman*, and Julie Breck as assistant editor. I needed some allies around me. Despite being far and away the biggest-selling monthly magazine in Britain, *Prima* had suffered circulation losses in recent years and Holger Wiemann, the UK managing director of G+J, was expecting me to turn it around – starting by making half a dozen redundancies.

It was a black day. I did what I had to do, then sat stunned that I had actually deprived people of their livelihoods. I didn't know how on earth I could ever summon the courage to leave my office to go home. Outside and in the loos, the remaining staff were in tears and no doubt calling me a prize bitch. I knew what that was like. Until recently I'd been one of them – the staff who had things done to them. So this was being an editor then? I wasn't at all sure it was for me but I could hardly go back to my old job as assistant editor on *Woman*. The only thing to do was go forward. The next day I gathered together the remaining staff and promised them that there would be no more job losses. We were going forward together. Within six months the downward slide in the circulation had been arrested and things were looking up. I was able to start hiring again. One of the people I took on was June Walton, a former showbusiness editor of *Today* newspaper who had worked extensively in the US as well, who was to prove herself a loyal ally.

But the turnaround meant working very long hours, often late into the night. Nanny Su had left us a year before for a job in the art world. She had been working as a nanny for over a decade and was desperate to find a job with more career progression. That's the problem with being a nanny, there is no opportunity for promotion. I understood her reasons but I found then, and have always found since, that having to hire a new nanny is the most god-awful part of being a working mother. And the only time when I have ever seriously thought about giving it all up and staying at home. How on earth do you choose someone to whom you can entrust your precious children?

Since the Labour Government came to power in 1997, childcare has been very much on the political agenda with some real improvements and tax breaks, but back in the early Nineties there was nothing. I had it said to me on many occasions that having children was a lifestyle choice and it wasn't up to employers or Government to do anything to assist women who wanted to 'have it all'. Even, presumably, if 'having it all' meant in mine and many other women's cases simply trying to keep a roof over your own and your children's heads.

The cheaper options of nurseries and childminders were always out of the question for me because the hours I worked were too long, so with each change of nanny I would hand over a small fortune to the agency who sent girls for interview and I would then painstakingly check and recheck all their qualifications and references myself. After they were hired I would be sure to pop back during the working day if I could possibly get away from the office, or have friends go round to the house and listen outside for suspicious noises or crying.

I have scared myself silly in the small hours of the night with apocryphal tales of cruel, feckless nannies although I've never come across one in real life. Never did one give me the slightest cause for concern about the way they cared for the children. Far from it, they brought an extra dimension of love and care into the family and we were all the better for it. I like to think I'm a good mother but I have never been an especially patient person, and the endless repetitive games that children love to play drive me bonkers after a bit. In their nannies the girls got a different perspective on life from people who were prepared to slow down to their speed. But the nannies were, of course, human and their own lives did get in the way. Trudi, who became pregnant, returned home to Kent when she had her little boy Billy to look after. Her replacement, Liz, got very homesick and went back to Australia after only eight months. I was in despair. We couldn't go on getting through nannies at this rate. I was conscious that the children had already suffered one major loss in their father. I didn't want them to go on suffering endless minor ones, too.

Then I heard, through a friend, of what she called the Rolls-Royce system of childcare, dreamed up – so legend among working mothers goes – by the QC Helena Kennedy. The theory is this. It's hard working in a private household – far harder than working in an office. Good nannies with a few years' experience under their belts don't want to live at their place of work as well. They want to be able to go to their own homes at night, to live with their boyfriends, or in their own flats. In London, at any rate, it's a seller's market and – not unreasonably – they get very resentful if they have to work late, night after night, because their employer is stuck in a meeting or has missed her train. (This rang a bell as I was constantly late home, rushing through the door, apologising profusely.)

The answer therefore is to hire the best live-out nanny you can find. Pay her as much as you can possibly afford (with tax and national insurance on top) and define her hours and her duties quite clearly. As clearly as you would for someone who works in your office. Then you also hire an au pair to do the housework and babysit the children for that gap between the nanny's going-home time and the time the employer gets home. The nanny is happy because she knows where her job begins and ends. And the au pair is ecstatic because she has time to go to her language classes, someone to talk English with during the day and she is not treated like a slave.

All too many au pairs are treated appallingly. The terms of an au pair's visa state that they come to this country to learn English. In return for their bed and board and pocket money they should do no more than four hours' light household duties per day plus babysitting. Yet I have come across many, many instances where au pairs are the sole child carers, working long, long hours and being burdened with responsibilities they are not ready for and can't cope with. It drives proper nannies (and good employers) mad to hear of such abuses but the cost of childcare is a crushing burden.

I was already struggling to pay one salary out of my own taxed income; I baulked at the idea of paying two. But other successful women I quizzed about the problem gave me the stern advice to spend as much as you can possibly afford on childcare because the peace of mind it gives you will enable you to increase your salary to match. It turned out they were right.

I hired Natasha, a trained and very experienced nanny who lived nearby in Crouch End, and who as a Sikh from a very traditional family would not have been able to take a live-in job. To back her up we had Maya from Slovenia. Au pair visas are only granted for one or maximum two years, so in time Maya was replaced by Patti from Spain, Caroline from France and then Marta from the Czech Republic. But Natasha was constant throughout. It was a fantastically successful arrangement and one I would recommend to anyone who can afford it and who needs to take their career seriously.

Even better, Natasha agreed to work late every Monday, which meant I could give the au pair Mondays off in return for her working Saturday mornings. Hooray! At last I had a few hours to myself to go shopping or swimming, or just lie in bed and recover from the week. I spent the first few weeks of my 'Free Saturdays' catching up on all the household stuff that had been neglected for so long; but then I decided to use the time to go riding.

All my life I'd loved horses, ever since my grandfather sat me on his knee and told me about the gee-gees. I was never much good at riding, being far too physically timid to jump or go at speed, but it did give me a sense of freedom and cleared my mind like nothing else. My pony, Trophy, had eventually died, of old age – while I was pregnant with Ellie, eight years previously – and I had been both too nervous and too busy to ride since. This was the perfect opportunity to get back in the saddle.

Every Saturday morning I would get up early, leaving the children with the au pair, and drive half an hour up the M1 to a riding stables. An hour's lesson, then a coffee, jump back in the car and get home to make lunch. It was like releasing a pressure valve in my head. Later when my friend Christina trained as a Riding for the Disabled instructor she told me that the benefits of riding go far beyond what might reasonably be expected from the exercise and coordination skills it encourages. Learning to work in harmony with another living creature can have a profoundly beneficial effect on the psyche, too. It calmed me down and for an hour I would think of nothing but how to stay with the horse. It cleared my mind of all the crazy stuff.

∞

And I needed it. Even though I had turned the circulation around, work was as demanding as ever. *Prima* had launched in the UK in 1986 and as the tenth anniversary approached I decided I wanted to do something really big to celebrate it. My idea was to get Cherie Blair to guest edit a special birthday edition. Tony was still leader of the opposition and there was a great deal of press interest in Cherie, who as a successful QC and mother of three school-age children was very far removed from the idea of conventional political wife. But she never spoke, never gave interviews and despite being the second most famous woman in Britain (after Princess Diana) was still very much an enigma.

I had met Cherie a couple of times at children's parties but didn't really know her. Fiona, however, was working for her as unofficial media adviser and promised to present my case to her. We didn't tell Alastair. We thought we'd wait and see what Cherie thought, then present him with a *fait accompli*.

Cherie loved the idea. She knew and liked the magazine and, having suddenly been thrust into the limelight, welcomed the opportunity to find out how the media worked from the other side.

Eventually Fiona and I owned up to Alastair what we were doing. He wasn't convinced it was a good idea but the three of us, Fiona, Cherie and myself, put up a united front so he had no choice. I wasn't sure my German bosses would really 'get it' either so I didn't bother telling them until the issue was nearly ready to go to press. In any case, I didn't want to give them the chance to say no. It seems incredible that no one realised what I was up to but in the magazine world smartly dressed, vaguely familiar-looking women are often seen hurrying up and down the corridors, so – apart from a couple of double-takes – we were able to keep her frequent visits to the office a secret.

Before her first visit, I briefed her by phone, then she came in for a meeting to outline her ideas for the magazine. She was late (I was to discover this was often the case). Stuck in court. She arrived in a whirlwind of smiles and apologies – a short white mac flung over her black court clothes and lugging a huge straw bag. The bag was upended on my desk and out came legal papers bound in red ribbon; a bottle of mineral water; gym kit; herbal tea bags and right at the very bottom some scraps of paper with her ideas for the magazine. I wasn't expecting much. The structure of a magazine is quite hard for an outsider to grasp. It should all look effortless but underneath there's quite a rigid formula to be followed. Somehow, though, she'd grasped the essentials and put together plans for a complete issue.

She wanted family meals that could be on the table half an hour after you walked through the door – and they had to be healthy. Fashion had to be trousers – she didn't like skirts. She decided to write a feature herself about how changes in employment law were affecting women; and she had even sketched out what she wanted for the knitting pattern. None of the press ever believed this but she is an accomplished knitter and not only designed the sweater we featured, briefing the knitting editor on stitches and yarn, but even checked the pattern and suggested improvements – something that even I as editor had never been able to do.

Nor was she interested in just garnering the publicity without doing all the work. She wrote all the headlines, checked all the proofs and for one month really did do everything an editor would do.

The only sticking point came when I felt the magazine needed an interview with Cherie as its focal point, but Fiona was adamant. Cherie wasn't doing interviews. Do one and you have to do them all. Eventually we reached a compromise, which was that a group of *Prima* subscribers would be invited to a tea party and given the opportunity to question Cherie directly. We didn't know how to wire everybody up with microphones so June and I sat there taking every question and answer down in shorthand and later transcribing it. Cherie was open and friendly and got on like a house on fire with the readers. She admitted to losing half a stone in weight after Tony became leader; that he cleaned all the family's shoes and occasionally cooked a meal, but wasn't on intimate terms with the washing machine. And on her life as a working mother lately thrust into the public eye, she said she sometimes felt as if she was 'just juggling all the balls in the air and I'm amazed that they don't all fall down at once'.

We also needed pictures of Cherie. There were none in existence except for family snaps and paparazzi shots which emphasised her wide mouth and huge eyes, making her look like a startled rabbit. As a result she loathed the thought of being photographed. I nagged, cajoled and lined up the *éminence grise* of fashion photography Anthony Crickmay to do a portrait. But she had never been professionally photographed before and was dreading it.

On the day of the shoot Cherie arrived at the studio clearly in a state. She looked as if she had been crying and this was the only time in our collaboration that she was unhelpful and unwilling. Carole Caplin had done her make-up and hair before she left home and Cherie refused at first to let our hairdresser and make-up artist touch it. Her aim was to be in and out and get the whole ghastly process over as fast as possible. The early Polaroids were awful. She looked tense and miserable. Eventually Crickmay declared a closed set and banished everyone but the make-up artist and the hairdresser who were sensitively retouching Carole's handiwork which was rapidly unravelling under the photographic lights. Fiona, the fashion editor and I sat downstairs in the kitchen drinking tea for two hours, wondering what on earth could be happening upstairs in the studio. Eventually Crickmay rejoined us brandishing Polaroids showing Cherie barefoot in leggings and a big sweater, looking completely herself –

relaxed, serene and really rather beautiful. 'Sometimes,' said Crickmay, rolling his eyes, 'you just have to bore them into submission.'

When the entire issue was ready to go to press I finally confessed to the managing director what I was up to. He was nonplussed but broadly supportive. Having grown up in Germany and spent most of his career in France, he was unaware of what the British tabloid press might make of it. Although the issue had been produced in conditions of utmost secrecy, news had started to leak out and we organised extra security at our warehouses as we'd heard that tabloid reporters might try to break in to get hold of advance copies. When the issue did go on sale it was a sensation. I was interviewed on *Newsnight* and in every national newspaper. The story was picked up in the US, where there was a great deal of interest in Cherie, and Crickmay's photos went all over the world.

Cherie loved the issue and even Alastair admitted it had been a good idea, showing Cherie as the person she really was without losing control and invading the family's privacy. Indeed there were many of the personal insights into her life that the press simply refused to believe. Even in those early days they wanted to see her as a Lady Macbeth figure. Years later, after the furore over her purchase of two flats in Bristol, when she spoke again of how hard it was 'juggle all the balls and keep them in the air' it was dismissed by some commentators as a cynical ploy for sympathy. But the truth was she'd been saying it since well before Tony was even elected.

And everyone thought I'd made up the bit about her being able to knit, and they disdained the idea that she would cook supper when she got in from work. But who did they think did it? Politicians aren't royalty – they don't have household staff. Like me – and probably like most of the female columnists who wrote about her – Cherie had a nanny to look after the children when she was at work, and when she got home – like most women – she started on the next shift.

Even so it was still a turning point in the perception of Cherie and also in my career. The shot of publicity came at the right moment for the magazine, and circulation rose again to new and dizzy heights. I was not only an editor but a supremely successful one. I replaced my old Marks & Spencer work suits with made-to-measure from couturiers Robinson Valentine – which meant overcoming my dislike of having clothes fitted on me. I bought my own Mulberry briefcase for the, by now not infrequent, trips by Eurostar to see Axel in Paris, and as a fortieth birthday present to myself, I traded in my old beat-up Audi for a sleek black Porsche – which was hugely imprac- tical and I sold it on within a year, but it did make me feel good at the time. I was elected chairwoman of the prestigious British Society of Magazine Editors. I had arrived . . .

∞

I didn't know it then but this part of the grieving process is called **restoration**, when you essentially fashion your- self a new life out of the ashes of the old one. I hadn't wanted to but I did it because I had to. And achieved a level of success I hadn't known I was capable of. The only trouble was that John wasn't there to see it. He was the only person I really wanted to share these things with. The only person whose approval I sought. But there was also the nagging doubt at the back of my mind. Would I have achieved all this if he were still alive? The answer is I didn't know then and I don't know now.

He was always 100 per cent supportive of my work but before his death I didn't have the drive to succeed. I had worked hard and had good jobs but when it came to making the final push for the top, protecting and conserving our home life had always seemed preferable. One glittering career with all the stresses and strains it imposed seemed enough for one household. But then he was so young when he became ill. Given more time could we have worked out a more equitable balance of power that allowed both our careers to prosper? Would it have been my turn to shine later on? Who knows?

In purely practical ways it was indescribably hard to make the biggest strides in my career as a single parent. It required a level of organisation and determination that makes me feel exhausted just to remember it. But I would be lying if I didn't also admit that in some ways it was easier than for my married friends. The need to provide for my family absolved me of a great deal of the energy-sapping guilt that goes with being a working mother.

∞

At the end of the photo shoot with Cherie, Crickmay took a quick snap of the two of us together. It hangs on the wall of my office still and spooks people because although we don't look especially like each other in the flesh – I am much taller – in this picture we could be twins. It captures a moment in time. Two hard-working, over-achieving Catholic girls trying to work out how to have a career, raise a family and survive in the shadow of their more famous husbands – whether alive or dead.

Chapter Six

∞

ZERO IMMUNITY

By 1997, five years after John's death, I'd refashioned our lives into something that – although it wasn't what John and I had originally planned – was really rather enviable. My career was soaring. The girls were happy and thriving at school. We spent every Christmas with Christina and her family in the Far East. And idyllic summer holidays in Ireland staying with our friends the Healys where Ellie and Hope learned to ride and seemed to be becoming as crazy about horses as I had always been.

On Guy Fawkes Night I rushed home from work with a few fireworks, and sausages for supper. Ellie was eight and Hope was four – both a bit young to enjoy loud bangs – so I was just making a gesture really. What's more they both had colds and even writing their names with sparklers in the night air wasn't going to hold much appeal.

A week later Hope was over her cold and back at school but Ellie couldn't seem to shake it off. On the Friday, I got Hope up in the morning but let Ellie sleep in. She always was a little dormouse and liked her rest. I told Natasha, our nanny, to call me and let me know how she was later on. I spent the morning at my office in the Docklands, reading proofs and copy for *Prima* and also overseeing work on the new magazines I had launched, *Your Home* and *Prima Baby*. Natasha rang to say that when Ellie had finally got up she wasn't really herself so she was going to take her to the doctor to see if she needed antibiotics. I wasn't remotely worried. Ellie had always been a healthy child, tall for her age and full of energy. Colds in the winter term were no cause for anxiety.

I had a quick lunch at the Oxo Tower on the South Bank with Sally Cartwright, publisher of *Hello!* magazine. We discussed the next year's magazines conference and the ways in which publishers and editors could work more closely together. Outside the restaurant, I called home to see how they'd got on at the doctor. Natasha told me that our GP – who'd looked after Ellie since she was a baby – was sure it was just a cold but had sent them to the local hospital, the Whittington, for a blood test to be on the safe side. I didn't like the sound of this, so rather than go back to the office I hailed a cab and went straight home, calling my PA on the way to rearrange my afternoon meetings.

As I walked through the door at home the phone was ringing. It was a consultant paediatrician at the Whittington. 'No need to worry but the blood tests look a little odd. Probably we just didn't get enough blood. Could you bring Ellie back to do the tests again?'

Leaving Hope with Natasha, I put Ellie – who by this time was exhausted and tearful – in the back of the car and drove back up to the Whittington. They took more blood from her arm and then, because she was so unnaturally tired, gave us a bed where she could lie down while we waited for the result. There was nothing in my mind. It was a total blank. The one terrible truth that was looming was so impossible, so unthinkable, that I refused to contemplate it. Ever since John's illness I'd had a horror of anything to do with blood, but I hadn't feared for Hope and Ellie – not while they were children anyway. Both John and his mother had been well into adulthood when they became ill.

Ellie used to ask me: 'Will I get leukaemia, too?' And I would answer, as her father's questions had been answered after his own mother died from leukaemia: 'I don't really think so but in any case by the time you are grown up the doctors will probably be able to treat you with just an injection, or something.'

At around 5pm the consultant called us in to see him. 'We can't say at this stage. But the blood tests don't look good. It may not be what we think . . . It may be something else . . .' I remember shrieking at him: 'What are the chances? . . . Just what are the bloody chances?'

They admitted Ellie onto a ward straightaway – in a side room, as her blood counts were so low they made her very vulnerable to infections from other children and their visitors – and started her on blood transfusions. She was puzzled, tired and fretful. Her arm with the needle in it hurt. I couldn't leave her for more than a few minutes at a time but I had to make arrangements for Hope – and the dog! Then, as now, mobile phones aren't allowed anywhere near medical equipment so I went outside to ring my mother.

'Hope has been dropped off at Terry's. You've got to collect her from there in the morning . . .'

She couldn't take it in. 'I don't understand,' she said dully. 'What's happening? Ellie can't have leukaemia. That was John. It won't happen again.'

'It can! It does! It has!' I screamed into the mobile phone. 'Don't argue with me – I have to get back to her.'

There was no bed for me and, in any case, Ellie couldn't bear for me to be apart from her – even to sit in the chair. I slept in my clothes next to her on the bed, my body curled around hers in a protective arc, careful not to touch the fat needle taped to her arm.

Over the next couple of days arrangements were made to transfer Ellie to Great Ormond Street Children's Hospital. The journey by ambulance kept being put off because the traffic was too heavy. I couldn't comprehend it but the truth was that Ellie was sinking so fast that even the half-hour journey between hospitals was risky.

Eventually we made it and she was admitted onto the ward which was actually a corridor of 12 individual rooms, each with a sort of airlock where medical staff and visitors could scrub up and put on a plastic apron to keep cross-infection to a minimum. The rooms were freshly decorated, each had its own bathroom, and the adaptations for barrier nursing meant that they afforded a great deal more privacy than a normal hospital ward. It was vastly superior to anywhere that John had been treated.

I was exhausted. I hadn't been home for three days and was still wearing the clothes that I'd had on when I'd rushed Ellie to the Whittington; my mobile phone battery was dead and worst of all I hadn't seen Hope since all this began. At age four, she had been passed around like a parcel from our nanny to my friend Terry then on to my mother who had collected her and the dog and taken them both home to Essex. If I couldn't hold her and reassure her then I at least needed to talk to her. As soon as Ellie was settled I set about trying to use the ward pay phone to call my mother and speak to Hope. But my British Telecom charge card – which I used whenever I travelled on business – didn't work. I discovered to my absolute horror that the pay phone required special cards that had to be bought from the shop – which was shut. It was the final straw! One child was dying, I couldn't speak to the other and some lousy phone company was coming between us.

I let rip like I'd never let rip in my life. All the fear and anxiety of the past few days came pouring out. The Assistant Administrator was sent for, then the Hospital Administrator himself. I screamed, I shouted, I threatened exposure in every major newspaper. The nurses and other parents looked on in horror as I made scene after scene. I was like a mad woman.

To the credit of the administration they had the phones sorted within days. Apparently no one else had complained before but the other parents on the ward thanked me for taking a stand – but for months afterwards some of the admin staff treated me warily whenever we met.

Ellie was given more blood transfusions, plus antibiotics and antifungals for the multiple opportunistic infections that were now raging through her body. Under general anaesthetic she had a Hickman line fitted to deliver drugs straight into a vein in her chest so she didn't have to keep being stabbed with needles. She also had a lumbar puncture – which involved fluid being taken from her spinal column – to establish just what sort of leukaemia she was suffering from.

The news wasn't good. The consultant, David Webb, sat me down and told me that she had Myelodysplastic Syndrome (MDS) which had caused a catastrophic collapse of the bone marrow. She was producing very few blood cells of any kind and those she was producing were undeveloped and malformed. MDS is one of the most rare blood cancers. It usually affects elderly people and can continue in a mild form for some time with few symptoms. But then it can morph suddenly into acute myeloid leukaemia, which is what we'd believed John had. The suspicion therefore was that John had in fact had MDS originally. Great Ormond Street contacted the Hammersmith for John's records – but even in the five years that had passed since John's death the state of medical knowledge had advanced further, and what could be gleaned from John's test results was of little help.

Attempts were made to track down his mother's medical notes, too, but that was pointless really, as she had died more than a quarter of a century before. All we knew was that like most other forms of leukaemia MDS is not normally thought of as hereditary and this was one of the few, possibly only, cases in the world of both father and child – and possibly grandmother – being affected.

I asked what the survival rates were and David Webb shook his head. Not good, he told me. Not good at all. I persisted. He told me that doctors don't like to talk in numbers in cases like this but – he groped for words – it just wasn't good.

Great strides have been made in the past few years in treating childhood leukaemia. Some forms have a more than 95 per cent success rate – which is wonderful and gives so much hope for the future that others will be conquered, too. But there are dozens of different kinds of leukaemia and MDS has proved to be one of the most intractable.

The plan was to put Ellie on a regime of five successive chemotherapy treatments over a period of six months. They would be intense, each course involving several intravenous treatments a day continuing for a week to 10 days, at which point her immunity would reach rock bottom making her vulnerable to all kinds of infections. Then as the platelets, red and white cells started to re-appear they would be hit again with another type of chemo, hopefully destroying the cancerous cells which always return first. It's a regime that was being used with some success to treat acute myeloid leukaemia in children but we never thought it would be a cure for Ellie. The main point for us was to get her into remission in the hopes that she would be strong enough to survive a bone marrow transplant.

A sample of my blood and one from Hope was analysed. Neither of us was a suitable match for her bone marrow. What was it with my family that no one ever matched anyone else? So it was back to trawling the Anthony Nolan Register, plus associated ones overseas, to try to find a match. To generate more publicity and encourage potential donors to come forward Alastair contacted several newspapers and we both went on ITN news to make appeals. I heard later that some 20,000 extra donors had come forward as a result of our publicity blitz, which has certainly meant that other lives have been saved. But no one matched with Ellie.

Ellie's first course of chemotherapy finished just before Christmas. I'd festooned her room with decorations and a minute tree – artificial, of course, fresh plant life not being allowed on the ward. And I'd been out to Selfridges and queued for hours to get Teletubbies and Spice Girls dolls (the must-have toys of 1997) for both girls, and even arranged through a mutual friend for Sporty Spice to send Ellie a card. It read:

> I'm so sorry to hear you are ill. Have a lovely Christmas and stay positive 'cos all you need is positivity. All the Spice Girls send their love and best wishes, we are praying for you. Girl Power! All my love forever. Melanie C (Sporty!)

Actually this backfired on me because although Ellie was used to Alastair appearing by her bedside not long after she'd seen him on TV, she simply couldn't believe that anyone so famous as Sporty Spice would actually write to her and was convinced I'd forged it!

Hope came up to stay and we were resigned to spending our Christmas in Great Ormond Street. But on Christmas Eve the consultant gave us the all-clear to go home provided I brought Ellie back the minute her temperature went up. I wasn't expecting to go home so there was no food in the house, but Terry cooked our Christmas dinner and then we went to Chequers for Tony and Cherie's Boxing Day party. Ellie's gorgeous auburn hair was falling out fast but we trimmed it into a 1920s bob and with a hat over the top it didn't look too bad. Carole Caplin took a photo of her with Tony and she was even able to go outside and play with the other children in the grounds. But on the drive back to London her temperature went up – a sure sign of another opportunistic infection – and by evening we were back on the ward.

It's incredible how quickly the most extreme situation develops its own routine. Ellie's illness and treatment followed a very different path from John's. He only spent the bare minimum of time in hospital – often discharging himself without permission in order to go to work. But Ellie's chemotherapy was far more intensive and we got home rarely. Effectively we lived at Great Ormond Street, with me sleeping on the sofa bed in her tiny room.

Unlike other parents on the ward, without a partner at home I had no choice but to send Hope to live with my parents. When it became clear that Ellie's treatment was going to take months, my mother arranged for Hope to go to the school in the village where she herself had taught for over 20 years. Hope dutifully attended and although she did a whole academic year there she insisted on wearing the uniform from her London school throughout to make it clear to everyone that this was a strictly temporary arrangement.

We spoke on the phone every night but being apart was agony for both of us. Each time we were able to be together I would give her the cardigan I'd been wearing and she would take it to bed with her at night so she could cuddle it and breathe in my scent. The next time we saw each other she would give it back, the fragrance all but worn off, and demand I hand over the one I was wearing, 'all smelled up' as she put it, to take to bed with her for the next few days or so. I wrote to her twice a week, even though she could barely read. Recently I found a letter I'd sent her which read:

Dear Hope. How rotten for you that you have this nasty cold. And how especially rotten that Ellie has been very ill so I haven't been able to come and look after you. I know Granny is very good at curing colds. She cured all mine when I was a little girl so I think she's the best possible person to be there if I can't. Just as soon as Ellie is a lot better I will come and see you and we'll have our half-term holiday then. Be brave. I love you very much. Mummy xxxxx (cold curing kisses).

She was too little to write back but would dictate her answers to us via my mother. Another I found was to her sister:

Dear Ellie, I love you so, so much I could just squeeze you but I can't squeeze you because you're not well. Love Hope x

Hope turned five in January 1998, but I couldn't be with her on her birthday because she'd sneezed earlier in the week. It didn't turn into a cold but I was so fearful of germs I stayed away anyway. Instead, with my mother's assistance I bought her a tiny, coal black pedigree kitten. Hope christened her Alice and, despite being the most bad-tempered and truculent cat to everyone else and frankly hostile to me, she was devoted to Hope, sleeping on her bed every night and submitting to all kinds of dressing-up games with feline good grace.

Provided there were no sneezes, though, and everyone had a normal temperature, on Fridays after school was over Hope and my mother would run down the road after school to the station and catch the train up to London and visit us in Great Ormond Street. The girls were always overjoyed to see each other and, provided Ellie was well enough, my mother would return home and Hope would stay over, sometimes sleeping on a camp bed wedged between Ellie and me. It was a tight squeeze and if Ellie needed attention in the night – which she usually did – we all woke up. But the nurses cheerfully clambered over us and did what they had to do and none of us felt quite so alone.

As Ellie became more settled and got to know the nurses, she was happy for me to take Hope home to sleep at weekends provided we were back by 10 in the morning. On a few blissful occasions we were all allowed home together and the girls relished the simple pleasures of sleeping in their own beds, eating home-cooked food and watching children's channels like Disney and Nickelodeon on cable TV.

But most nights Ellie needed chemotherapy drugs, antibiotics or blood transfusions through her Hickman line so she would sleep hooked up to a drip-stand with a monitor which would bleep when the bag needed changing. Some nurses were expert at creeping in just before the bleep went off and changing the bag; others were slower and I'd be woken by the bleeping every half an hour or so and have to get up and go in search of someone to hook up more drugs or blood.

In the morning, Ellie often slept in after these disturbed nights so I'd shower in her tiny bathroom and dress in one of the two outfits I kept on the ward. Then I'd nip down to the cafeteria for a coffee and a newspaper and to buy Ellie a little box of her favourite cereal Cheerios and a bottle of fruit juice in the hopes that she might eat some breakfast.

Getting Ellie to eat was a nightmare. She was frequently nauseated from the chemotherapy or had a temperature from the infections that attacked when her resistance was low, plus she often suffered from mucositis – an inflammation of the lining of the mouth and throat that made swallowing very painful. The hospital food that came up on trays from the kitchens didn't appeal to her at all so I mostly lived off that myself. There was a kitchen on the ward that parents could use to prepare food and I would sometimes boil her some plain pasta and grate some cheese over it which was still her favourite meal. But although hygiene regulations were strict – no raw meat or fish, no eggs; all dishes and cutlery to be put in the dishwasher on the highest temperature; all surfaces swabbed down with bleach – you could never really trust the new parents.

In the intense and literally febrile world of the ward new parents were a nuisance. They arrived, as you might expect, in a terrible state – their child had just been diagnosed with leukaemia, after all. But unlike us old hands whose children had particularly intractable forms of blood cancer, nine times out of ten these parents and their children would receive the welcome news that it was a very treatable form and as soon as the child was stable they'd be off to their local hospital for chemotherapy which although nasty – and not something you'd wish on anyone – would almost certainly be entirely successful.

In the few days they spent with us they never got the hang of life in our zero immunity world. They would sneeze; appear on the ward with cold sores; barge in and out of the children's rooms without scrubbing up. Time and time again I would go into the kitchen and see a fellow long-stay parent grimly loading the dishwasher with what looked like sparkling clean plates. 'New parent,' she would say. And I'd know that meant that someone new on the ward had helpfully unloaded the dishwasher but not known she had to scrub her hands first.

With our children hovering between life and death we lived in fear of the sort of bugs and germs that healthy kids brush aside. An outbreak of food poisoning would have wiped out every child on the ward. The long-stay parents all became afflicted by a sort of obsessive-compulsive disorder, endlessly washing and rewashing dishes and repetitively wiping down surfaces. 'Think I might have touched my nose,' was all the explanation that was needed for someone to re-do a task that had just been completed.

Maggie the ward sister ran the ward with a rod of iron. Known for her fearsome bed-making technique, I was constantly having to burrow through the bags of dirty washing to retrieve Ellie's special teddy Apricot who would get swept up in the laundry. Even so, she was always Ellie's favourite. She kept a league table of the others – Bernie, David, Sue, Tracey, Steve and Eileen – checking out who was best at blood tests, or drip changing, and took mischievous delight in relaying to them their different positions in the league.

Eventually Ellie became very fond of all the nurses and would let me spend an hour or so away from her. I would rush to my car, which I kept at great expense in a private garage around the corner, whiz home and boil her some pasta in my own kitchen. While it was cooking I would deal with the post that had accumulated in our absence and do any other pressing tasks and then drive back – as I had done for John – with a plate of food on the front seat of the car next to me. She might then, if I was lucky, eat about a quarter of it.

The children were weighed every week, which they all hated. Once when the inflammation in Ellie's mouth was so bad she could barely swallow, the doctors asked if they could give her a naso-gastric tube to get nourishment down her. I agreed, of course, but then was horrified as I had to hold her down while they inserted the tube. It took them half an hour and at the end we were both sobbing. I couldn't stand it. I called the nurses back and insisted they take the tube out again. Then I got down on my knees beside her bed and begged her to swallow at least enough to stay alive.

We tried every cream going to soothe Ellie's poor lips, but it was one of John's former colleagues from the *Daily Mirror*, writer Noreen Taylor, who provided the answer.

Incredibly glamorous, she wafted onto the ward, all long blonde hair and designer draperies, and produced from her handbag a tube of Elizabeth Arden Eight Hour Cream. Ellie loved it and miraculously it did seem to do the job of healing her lips. After that Noreen was assiduous in dropping off a tube whenever she was passing.

And if I had little else at that point, I did have the support of my family and friends who had swung into action like a well-oiled machine. My aunt Carol drove up from Essex every Tuesday to sit with Ellie teaching her to knit and sew. Alastair came by twice a week and would stay and read to her for hours regardless of what was going on back at Number 10. Once though he did get a pager message to say he was needed urgently and ran out of the hospital still wearing the plastic earrings that Ellie had stuck on his ears for a joke. Tessa Jowell, who was a health minister at the time, would cause consternation when she popped in with fabulous picnics of Marks & Spencer food. And Cherie would come and sit on Ellie's bed and chat, confusing the ward teacher no end as he was convinced he knew her from somewhere but he just couldn't work out where.

I did everything I could to bring the outside world – albeit scrubbed and gowned – into Ellie's little room but more than anything else she just longed to go back to school. Her teacher and classmates were wonderful, visiting when they could and sending her long letters every week describing all their activities, but the risks of infection were too great to allow her to mix with a whole class of children.

Great Ormond Street has its own school but the children on the leukaemia ward were too vulnerable even to join that so they had their own lessons. Every morning that she was well enough Ellie studied alongside others who were about the same age including Joe, Bradley and Georgie. Despite the fact that they were all bald from their chemo, and all had Hickman lines which were permanently attached to drip stands which they dragged up and down the corridor in their wake, they were still just regular kids, too.

Bradley was a holy terror, famous throughout the hospital for the time he rang up a limo firm and sent them to get enough takeaway pizza for the entire ward. His mother used to babysit Posh Spice when she was baby Victoria Adams (now, of course, Victoria Beckham). It was the height of the Spice Girls fame and Posh sent Bradley all sorts of Spice Girls memorabilia, which he ruthlessly traded with Ellie who was prepared to believe that Bradley had access to a Spice Girl even if she didn't think I did. In return she handed over the stuff she received from Arsenal. The football club are based just down the road from our home in North London and – I discovered – are assiduous in keeping in touch with sick children in the area. Although Ellie had no interest in football and had never been to a match, the school alerted them to her illness and they sent her signed memorabilia and a long personal letter signed by manager Arsene Wenger. Neither of us even knew who he was but Bradley did and was happy to take it off her hands.

Georgie was two years older than Ellie and had one of the most curable forms of childhood leukaemia but, of course, a 95 per cent success rate still means that 5 per cent don't make it. It's a numbers game and you can be on the wrong side of the numbers. Georgie had been ill on and off since she was three, which meant that she had been in and out of hospitals all that time. She quickly taught Ellie the ropes of life with leukaemia, advising: 'When your hair falls out don't bother with the wigs – they itch.' Georgie's mother Nicola Horlick – who had four other children – had earned the soubriquet 'superwoman' because she also commanded a £1.5 million salary from her job in the City.

I was intrigued as to how she held down any job at all as she'd been accompanying Georgie in and out of hospital for eight years. My employers were being generous with time off and my deputy editor Louise Court was doing a fantastic job but I knew I had to get back to work. I didn't know how long Ellie would be ill but we only had my salary to live on and illness is expensive. Nicola's advice was succinct: 'When you're at work concentrate on that fully and don't fret about how you should be with Ellie. When you're with Ellie don't give work a thought.' I never quite achieved that but I did get back to work. In the mornings while Ellie had lessons, I would put a jacket over the skirt and T-shirt I usually wore on the ward and go to the office. Then in the afternoons I would return to the hospital, armed with mobile phone, laptop and pager (to alert me for phone calls), and sit beside her, ploughing my way through copy and proofs.

I would also work late into the night while Ellie slept and even devised a brand new health magazine which I called *Vital*. It was only published once but was a sellout. People would ask me how I could possibly think of work at a time like that. My answer was, how could I not? Everything else was too awful to contemplate.

I knew the outlook wasn't good but John had lived two years from diagnosis. I was hopeful that Ellie would do the same or even better. Generally, children are stronger, recovering from chemo faster, and great strides are being made all the time. When Ellie asked if she was going to die like her Daddy I told her the truth, that childhood leukaemia is way more treatable than the adult kind. Sometimes she would persist: 'But what if I do die?' 'Then you'll go straight from my arms to your Daddy's,' I told her. 'You won't feel a thing except being wrapped in love.'

In the early days after Ellie's diagnosis, one thing that escaped my frazzled brain altogether was that as chair-woman of the British Society of Magazine Editors I was supposed to be hosting the end-of-year awards dinner at The Dorchester Hotel. Sharon Ring, then editor of the celebrity magazine *OK!*, was primed to cover for me, and as I dithered, the nurses decided that there was little enough glamour on the ward, and all but pushed me out the door. I had nothing to wear, but the *Prima* team met me in the foyer with a deep red silk evening dress that had been featured in the magazine plus underwear and shoes that they had bought for me, guessing my size and taste. I sat like a zombie in the hotel room while they did my hair and make-up. Then as my name was announced by the Toastmaster, and Sharon Ring hovered by the side of the stage ready to step in if need be, I walked to the microphone, took a deep breath and started reading from the autocue.

It passed in a blur. For an hour I handed over trophies to the award-winning editors, including Gill Hudson for *Maxim*, Alex Finer for *Hot Air* and Dr Alun Anderson of *New Scientist*, introduced the stand-up comedian Arthur Smith and hosted a raffle in aid of the charity Winston's Wish, which offers bereavement counselling to children. As I reached the end of my script I looked up and registered for the first time the 650 editors and publishers who comprised the audience. And then they were all on their feet, cheering and clapping, and giving me a standing ovation as I stood there with tears pour-ing down my face. I hung around afterwards to drink champagne with the awards judges – Ian Hislop, Amy Jenkins, Roy Greenslade and Trevor Beattie – but couldn't really settle to it.

After about half an hour I slipped out, pulled on my old tracksuit, handed back all my borrowed finery and headed back to Great Ormond Street where the nurses had made up my sofa bed for me and wanted to hear all about my night out.

∞

Ellie's course of chemotherapy took far longer than we had initially hoped. After each bout it took weeks rather than days for her blood counts to come back and during the vulnerable phase she suffered horrible opportunistic infections, from ringworm on her skin to aspergillus in her chest, and then she developed a perforated bowel. Each crisis was terrifying. Although she needed treatment from other specialists we couldn't risk contact with patients in other parts of the hospital for fear of cross-infection, so she would have x-rays and scans after everyone else had gone home and I would push her wheel-chair down the dark and ghostly corridors. As far as possible I gave her all her medicines myself, crushing tablets in a pestle and mortar brought in from home to make them easier to swallow, and running out to the shops for Calpol to replace the nasty-tasting hospital issue para-cetamol. She wouldn't allow anyone but me to administer her eye drops. Her fourth bout of chemo took an age to get over and when she finally rebuilt her resistance, our consultant suggested we go home for a break before returning for the fifth and final bout. As he had done when he sent us home at Christmas, he was always care-ful to balance the extreme life-saving measures Ellie was going through with maintaining some semblance of quality of life.

It was agreed that she would go home on 10 June 1998. It would only be for three weeks and Ellie would have to spend most of every day in the Whittington Hospital but she would be able to sleep in her own bed, eat home-cooked food. See her sister. Watch *Sabrina the Teenage Witch* on cable TV. Phone up her school friends. Just a normal nine-year-old living with her mum and her sister. I brought into the hospital ward the soft-sided bags we'd originally taken to Japan and now used for her packing whenever she got home-leave.

Bad news. Ellie's temperature was up again although only slightly. The doctors ummed and aahed and said she'd better stay just one more night. Ellie was upset but Maggie the ward sister came and reassured her that the only reason she had to stay was that once her bed had been given up – even if only for three weeks – then another child would move into it for the duration so they wanted to be sure that she really was well enough to be at home.

The day staff went home and the night staff came on duty. To cheer ourselves up we decided to order a take-away. When she was feeling well enough and had an appetite Ellie liked nothing more than to order from a service she'd recently discovered, called Restaurant Express, which sent a car to the restaurant of your choice and picked up your order. Part of the fun was poring over the menus and tonight she decided it was to be Greek again – her current passion.

We ordered so much that it took me two trips down to the lobby to collect it. There was hummus, pitta bread, several main courses plus Greek salad, and baklava for dessert. Luckily Bernie, one of Ellie's favourite nurses, was on duty, a pretty young Irish nurse known for her prodigious appetite, so we were fairly sure she would be able to help us out with our feast. Ellie, Bernie and I ate our fill and then we watched *ER* on the television above the bed. Not surprisingly Ellie wasn't interested in watching a hospital drama on TV so she took herself off to her bathroom with a book about ballet and lay in the bath reading. She emerged as *ER* was finishing, having read the whole book from cover to cover but still voracious for more stories, so we settled down for her regular bedtime story. During our eight months living together in that tiny room

– not even 10 feet square – Ellie and I had whiled away the hours reading our way together through almost every children's classic. That night we were finishing *Swallow-dale*. We had read *Swallows and Amazons* by Arthur Ransome and progressed on to the sequel. In Ellie's imagination she had sailed every voyage with the crew of the *Swallow*, camped overnight with them on Wildcat Island and taken part in every adventure.

Then, as she did every night, she said her prayers: 'God bless Mummy. God bless Daddy up in Heaven. God bless Hope who doesn't understand why she can't be here with us. And God bless me. Please don't let me have any nasty dreams tonight. Amen.' Kneeling up on her bed, the light from the bedside table reflecting off the down of fine red-gold hair that had only just started to grow back after months of chemotherapy, she prayed to a God who seemed to have forgotten all about us.

∞

She didn't want to go to sleep that night. She never did. Her hospital bed was board hard with the obligatory plastic sheet to protect it. We agreed that I would go home to sleep and get the house ready for her which meant she could sleep on the sofa bed with my duvet rather than scratchy hospital blankets. This was normally against the rules but the night staff took the view that she could have a special treat. She was nearly home anyway. Then I kissed her and settled her in bed, and set off for home.

At the nurses' station I stopped to chat, and while I was there Ellie ran out of her room calling: 'Mummy, Mummy.' I can see her now in her red dressing gown, precisely belted, matching her red slippers, and I had a moment of panic before I saw her cheeky grin, her hand with its long nails painted in Chanel pink flying to her mouth to cover it. She had grown her nails to compensate for her hair falling out and delighted in manicuring them and painting them different shades.

I ran up the corridor to see what was wrong and she whispered to me that I'd left my mobile phone in her room, switched on – which was strictly forbidden – and it was ringing. Conspiratorially we returned to her room and I answered the call. It was Terry to say she was coming home from work, late in a taxi. Should she detour and give me a lift?

I hurried Ellie back into bed, kissed her and settled her again, and set off to rendezvous with Terry. On the way I exchanged a few words with the Senior Registrar on duty that night. He'd had a rough time with a very sick baby on the ward, but by the time we got to the exit we were laughing and joking, and congratulating each other on how well Ellie had recovered from her latest scare and how much she was looking forward to going home.

In the morning, I didn't hurry. We'd been so late the night before that I doubted Ellie would even be awake by the time I got there. I called Terry and said I'd give her a lift on my way to the hospital. She was making coffee when I arrived to pick her up at 9am, but when we sat down to drink it we realised the milk was off so we abandoned that idea and headed out to the car. As we did so my pager went off. It read: 'Ring Ward. Urgent.' I jumped in the car and drove. Terry rang the ward and a nurse said: 'Just get here as soon as you can.'

The trip from Crouch End to Great Ormond Street is about four miles. In the London rush hour that can easily take 40 minutes – we did it in 20. I double-parked outside the hospital, throwing Terry the keys to park the car, then ran up all four flights to the ward. It seemed as if every doctor or nurse in the hospital was gathered in the corridor. In the confusion I met the eye of a young Chinese House Officer and saw she was crying.

'Is she alive? Where's Ellie? I want to see her.'

The consultant took an impossibly long breath. 'Technically, yes, she's alive. But now you're here . . .'

Hands grabbed me and pulled me into the interview room. There were nurses, tissues; the consultant David Webb spoke: 'We'd like your permission to stop trying to resuscitate her. We think it's been pointless for some time.'

I had one thought. 'I want my baby. I want her. Let me see her. Let me go to her now.'

'You can't,' they said. 'The room's a mess. We did everything we could but a fungal infection invaded her aorta and severed it. She haemorrhaged to death. It was very quick. But messy. You don't want to see her like that.'

Oh, but I did. I'd given birth to her and there was nothing about her life, or her death, that I didn't want to be part of. I struggled free of their restraining hands and staggered down the corridor to her room. They were right. It was a mess.

Apparently she had woken just before nine, and while her nurse, Kate, made the bed she had gone to the bathroom to wash and dress ready to go home. In the bathroom she had started coughing and brought up some blood. She came out and said: 'What's happening?' Kate pressed the emergency buzzer and all the doctors who were on their ward rounds rushed into the room. The cardiac unit was called, and Intensive Care. But it was too late.

I looked at the little room we had lived in for eight months, her pictures on the walls, our bags placed ready to be packed, and everything was flung about. Her blood was streaked up the walls, chairs were tipped over, sinister-looking machinery had been dragged in. It was the scene of a devastatingly horrible accident. Yet in the middle of it all, she lay serene on her bed. The baby I had given birth to just nine and a half years before. The same golden hair. Her face slightly puffy and bruised as it had been from the forceps and streaks of blood down her face.

Terry took over and rang Alastair and Jeremy who arrived within minutes. She tried to ring my parents who were en route for a holiday in Cornwall with Hope, but we couldn't raise them on the mobile phone. Fr Anthony was on his way, but the Great Ormond Street chaplain arrived before him and took me back into the interview room so the nurses could straighten the room.

Eventually they let me back in to see her – tidied up but already cold and gone from our world. Her eyes were still slightly open – she never could sleep with her eyes fully shut. She was no longer with us but was now free, I hoped, from all the pain. I talked to her a little, held her hand, kissed her. Then I started to pack. She was leaving hospital after all. Just not the way we'd intended. I, her mother, was supposed to collect her. But as it turned out she'd gone with her father instead. I packed her bags all the same. It was something to do.

Chapter Seven

∞

LIVING ON THE

SEABED

I had to get to Hope. With Ellie gone the only thing I could think of was that I had to hold and touch my one remaining child. But we didn't know where in Cornwall she was. The contact details they had left were vague and we still couldn't get through on the mobile phone.

I had to get to her.

I packed a small bag with Ellie's bloodstained pyjamas, the book she'd been reading and the teddy bear she called Apricot. Despite the fact that it was June and the weather was sunny, I felt cold so I put an old riding jacket over my business suit. Then Jeremy and I went to Paddington and caught the train to Plymouth. While we were on the train Alastair called up Geoff Lakeman, the *Daily Mirror*'s man in the West Country, and asked him to meet us at the station. His encyclopaedic knowledge of the area meant that he knew where all the rental property was likely to be and could make a good guess as to where we would find my parents and Hope.

Jeremy and I sat on the train in silence. I stared out of the window at the same scenery I had passed on my journey down to Devon nearly two decades before when I had been starting out as a journalist and just before I met John for the first time. It felt somehow fitting to be making the journey again. Like a pilgrimage.

Geoff had known us both when we were just trainee journalists. He and his wife Joy had fed us when our

meagre salaries ran out, subsidised us by paying generously for tips of stories Geoff could follow up and had
helped John get his first big scoop into the *Mirror*. Now
he was waiting for me on the station concourse, choking
back tears.

Incredibly he found the cottage within an hour and
dropped me and Jeremy at the gates. I walked up the path.
Hope ran out to meet me shouting: 'Mummy, Mummy,
you came after all.' Then she stopped, saw my face and
burst into tears. My mother was at the kitchen window;
she looked puzzled and then – as realisation dawned –
appalled.

It was too late in the day to travel back to London so
we stayed the night, sleeping on sofas in our clothes as
I'd only packed Ellie's belongings, which I couldn't bear
to be parted from. We hadn't packed anything for
ourselves. Then in the morning Jeremy and I took Hope
back to London and once again entered into that strange
no-man's land between a death and a funeral.

Again Jeremy registered the death and started making
the funeral arrangements. And again friends descended
on the house to care for me. If anyone had told me after
John's death that things could be even worse I would
never have believed them. But it was. I was in such a state
of shock, and so was everyone else, that we couldn't think
straight, or organise anything to eat or beds for the people
who were staying over to sleep on.

Christina, who was living in Hong Kong by this time,
had simply gone to the airport as soon as she heard the
news and got on the first plane out. She arrived before
dawn the next morning and quickly sized up the chaos
and lack of food and comforts in the house. As soon as
the shops were open she went out and bought spare duvets
and Marks & Spencer salads, sandwiches and wine to keep
everyone going.

Our anguish was all but unbearable. My cousin De

came to stay and Hope made her sleep in Ellie's bed in the bedroom they used to share. But, terrified that De too would be gone in the morning, Hope constructed an intricate web of dressing gown belts, scarves and ribbons lashed between the head- and tailboards, designed to prevent her from escaping. In order to sleep De had to wriggle down under the web and lie flat on her back. Hope would then check on her throughout the night to make sure she hadn't vanished like the rest of her family seemed to be doing.

I barely slept at all. Every time I shut my eyes I teetered on the brink of a terrible abyss and would wake again – screaming. My GP very reluctantly doled out a few sleeping tablets with stern warnings to make them last because she wouldn't give me any more, ever! Did she think I might kill myself? Of course she did. Everyone did. They were watching me like hawks.

And however bad it was I knew that the worst was still to come. The problem was not that I might be so despairing that I would want to kill myself – not at this point anyway – but that I had to cut through the fog of shock and denial and force my brain to comprehend what had happened. I needed to see Ellie again for the last time. And I knew that Hope had to see her too, otherwise she might always wonder whether in fact it was some sort of trick and that Ellie was still alive and might come back to us. But how could I make it real for Hope without her being traumatised as I had been by seeing John's body? I didn't know what to do except I knew I had to do something because I only had a week until the funeral.

Most people I asked were firmly opposed to the idea. You and Hope should try to remember Ellie as she was before she got ill, they said. But then I consulted my friend Carmel who's Catholic like me but spent much of her childhood in Ireland, where to my mind they have a much more accepting view of death. She reassured me that seeing the body was an entirely normal and expected part of mourning in Ireland. There, she explained to me, the body would be brought back to the house and every relative and friend – children as well as adults – would be expected to visit and pay their respects. She and her sister and eight brothers had taken part in this ritual many times over and she said it wasn't morbid but actually a very comforting way to say goodbye.

I didn't think it would be possible to bring Ellie's body home. I didn't know how to arrange it. Instead Hope and I went out for lunch with Carmel and all her children, and Carmel's sister Sheila and her kids, and we had pizza then walked down the road to Great Ormond Street in a great long procession – I think there were about 12 of us in total. At the hospital we asked to see Ellie's body, which was being kept in the morgue. We had to wait about 15 minutes while everything was prepared for us but there were toys and books for the children in the ante-room. And everyone was quite calm and happy.

I warned Hope that Ellie would look different, now that her soul had left her body, and not as she had done when she was alive. And she seemed to accept that. Eventually we were shown in to a small chapel where Ellie's body had been arranged on a little bed. She was wearing a pair of her own clean pyjamas and the embroidered cloche hat she always wore to cover her baldness. One of the nurses from the ward had been down and repainted her nails so they were fresh and pink and pretty.

It was all very peaceful and not at all distressing. Carmel's eldest daughter Maud, who was almost exactly the same age as Ellie, dropped to her knees and began to say the prayers of the rosary. One by one all the children joined in with her, gathering protectively around Hope in their centre.

Then they stood up and took it in turns to kiss Ellie and say goodbye. Outside on the street the sun was shining. We bought ice-cream and took the children to play on the swings in nearby Coram Fields. They talked about Ellie all afternoon, imagining what she would be saying and doing if she was playing there with them. And when I half-shut my eyes and listened to them chattering I could imagine she was.

∞

With a child there is very much less to organise in the run-up to the funeral. There were no bank accounts to be unfrozen, no will to be read, no accounts to be sorted out. Ellie had made her First Communion the year before so I arranged that she should be clothed in her long white Communion dress and the children from her class at school would sing *Like A Sunflower*, the hymn she had chosen then as her favourite. It conjured up images for me of her golden head nodding sleepily in the summer sun.

Christina, practical as ever, was more concerned about what a sight I looked. Eight months living on hospital food and sleeping on a sofa bed had left me gaunt and slightly hunched from a bad back. I hadn't been to the hairdresser, or the dental hygienist, or bought new clothes in that time. I was a mess.

'You're not burying your daughter looking like that,' she announced and fixed for me to get my hair done. Then she took me shopping and I bought a pale blue outfit to wear as I'd decided black was inappropriate for a child's funeral. For Hope I bought a simple white cotton frock and a hairband decorated with flowers.

∞

How to describe the day of her funeral? It was incredibly beautiful and at the same time utterly terrible that such a day should dawn at all. Hundreds of people came. The sun shone. Ellie was carried into church by her three real uncles and her fourth unofficial uncle, Alastair. Terry spoke the eulogy. Another friend Cathy – a professional violinist – played music ranging from *Colours of the Wind* from Disney's *Pocahontas* – Ellie's favourite as she had been invited to the premiere – to a heart-stopping rendition of Vaughan Williams' *Lark Ascending*. Carmel read a poem she had written about our holiday in Ireland the previous summer, and which was later to win an award. It conjured up the glorious time just months before Ellie got ill, when there was no sign of what was to come.

> Your footsteps crunch the lane, your laughter
>   echoing out to the horses.
> You are raising fences, lugging planks, tipping
>   tyres for your makeshift
> Arena. A happy girl show-jumper in pink
>   Wellingtons and a riding hat
> From which your glorious red hair is still conspir-
>   ing its startling escape.

All of her year at school came and each child brought a hand-picked posy which they placed at the foot of her coffin until the whole of the church floor around her was carpeted with blossoms, especially poignant as she hadn't been allowed any flowers near her for the whole of her illness. They had also compiled a book of memories in which each classmate had written something about her or drawn a picture.

One little girl wrote: 'Ellie was a very good friend to me. She played with me when I was lonely, she helped me when I was stuck. She was always nice when we spent time together. She never got cross or in a bad mood. Ellie was very clever and she nearly always got full marks. I remember in reception class the teacher said: "Do you know who's my angel?" And it was Eleanor. I will always remember her.'

I was dazed and slightly spaced out but I held tight onto Hope and we got through it. Only as the coffin, covered with pink flowers, was lowered into a grave alongside John's did I feel my knees buckle and my father caught me before I fell. Afterwards Terry, faithful as ever, had again organised a reception and barbecue at her house. And the same people stood around as they had six years previously, talking this time of Ellie as well as John, while Hope ran between them revelling in all the attention.

And again the feeling after the funeral of what else is there but to go back to work? This time it was Christina who scooped me up and insisted Hope and I return with her to Hong Kong. So we booked tickets, packed our bags and headed off for Heathrow. Only to find that we were in such state, we had misread the time of the flight and missed it.

Christina, the former Wall Street stockbroker turned most organised woman in the world, and I, magazine editor and former astrophysicist, stood at the check-in desk and stared uncomprehendingly at our tickets. We had miscalculated the 24-hour clock thinking that 1800 hours was 8pm not 6pm. How could we have been so stupid? Both of us? Worse, we had no idea what to do except I knew I couldn't go back home to the empty echoing house. Christina pulled out a bottle of the herbal tonic Bach Rescue Remedy® from her bag and we both took a mighty swig and then burst into tears. Seeing us crying, Hope joined in as well.

Somehow the whole story came out and before we knew what was happening the girl at the British Airways check-in had ushered us along to the business class lounge – even though we had economy tickets – and got Hope a drink and a snack while she fixed for us to get on a flight with another airline.

When the boarding announcement was made a flight attendant came and collected us, and saw us right to the gate – obviously convinced that we were so distraught that we would get lost again in the airport. Which was probably right. In amongst all the dreadful things that were happening these little pockets of kindness I encountered – often from strangers whose names I never knew and whom I never got to thank properly – nonetheless helped a bit.

Back at her home in Hong Kong, Christina's equanimity returned and she set about rebuilding me physically – even if she couldn't manage it mentally. I was made to swim and ride and had my back seen to and my teeth scraped. I even started to sleep a little. Hope played with Christina's boys and learned to swim, which gave me several heart-stopping moments as she plunged fearlessly into the pool and struck out for the opposite side. Time and time again I dived in to retrieve her – once so hastily that the book I was reading went in with me. It seemed to me entirely possible that I could lose two children in the space of two weeks. That was the way my luck was running.

We stayed 10 days then headed back home. As with John's death I was back at my desk within three weeks. In the years since, I have often been asked, as an employer, how much time off someone needs when they've been bereaved. Obviously, I don't think there would be much point in anyone trying to work between the death and the funeral – even if they could. And afterwards I did need a short break of a week or so to recover my strength. But I wasn't ill or mad (well, not very), just very sad, and I don't really see that time off work is a cure for that. Rather the reverse is true, that familiar routines and mental distractions can be a relief. Better, by far, to get back to work as soon as possible and save the employer's good will for the time that will definitely come six or so months down the line when you hit the seabed of despair and can barely make it out of bed, let alone do a day's work.

∞

There is no escaping the seabed phase. Nor can you alleviate it, however much you might be prepared for its coming. You can't go round it, or over it. There is only one way and that's through it. Five months after John's death, my plunge into depression was triggered by Hope's birth. But this time around, even without the hormonal upheaval and even knowing everything I had learned since, in the months after Ellie's death both Hope and I travelled remorselessly down that path again. I went back to work and Hope returned to live at home and went back to her original school. To outward appearances we looked like we were coping as we went through the motions of normal life, but with every day that passed we sank lower and lower into despair.

I could see it happening but was powerless to stop it. I could see no point, no future in anything. If John could die and Ellie could die, why wouldn't Hope die, too? Everyone else was dying around me. My father was diagnosed with cancer – for the fourth time. This time in his stomach. My relationship with Bill, which had briefly reignited when he moved to London and spent some time looking after the house for me while I was in the hospital with Ellie, spluttered and died on my return from Hong Kong. He'd met someone else, he told me. He hadn't thought there was any future for us . . .

Fine! I never thought there was any future for me either.

Then the dog died. Rosie, the feisty little Norfolk Terrier that John and I had bought as a puppy, 14 years earlier. No more than six inches tall, she was bad-tempered, virtually untrainable, frequently bit people and both John and I adored her. All through John's illness when it would have made more sense to send her to my mother's as we were battling with his lack of immunity, we kept her with us at home. Sometimes her company had been the only solace either of us could find. Walking her for hours on the Heath had brought us some measure of calm. Now she was gone, too. I felt utterly abandoned and a total failure. Everyone, everything I loved died. I didn't want to be the last one left alive. I wanted to die, too.

There's a sort of unwritten rule – or maybe it's written somewhere, I don't know – that you shouldn't talk about suicidal feelings for fear of encouraging them in other people – legitimising them if you like. But I'm prepared to place a bet that there is no one who has been profoundly bereaved who hasn't thought – however briefly – about joining the other side. I know I did.

Medically, Ellie's case appeared to be unique, her condition so rare that it was impossible to predict what this might mean for Hope. The doctors refused to speculate and, to this day, I too refuse to speculate. What is the point of me with no medical training trying to guess what the implications are – or are not – for Hope, when people who have spent lifetimes researching this area say they have no idea?

But whether or not she was to contract leukaemia I had no very real expectation of Hope surviving to adulthood. The state of my mind being what it was, I could barely believe it that she woke up each morning. I was convinced that she would be taken in the night. I didn't know how but I was sure she would follow John and Ellie (and the dog) – and I had no intention of burying another child. I would be gone, too. I even knew how I would do it. I would drive to Epping Forest and run a hosepipe from the exhaust into my car. I did wonder a bit actually how you fixed it on but I was fairly sure it would be relatively straightforward for someone with a science degree. Knowing that I would kill myself rather than suffer any more wasn't a frightening thought. It was a very comforting one. I didn't confide it in anyone. But one person did guess.

George Pitcher had worked on *The Observer* with John but later left to set up his own PR business. After John's death he rang me up and said: 'There's not much I, or anyone else, can do but if I take you out for a drink once in a while it can't hurt and it might help.' And so he did. George is very happily married and his beautiful wife Mobs is luckily secure and confident enough not to mind that every few weeks or so, I would meet George after work and we would go to El Vino's, sink a bottle of wine, or two, and talk things over. I was usually home by 8pm so our evenings didn't even cause great babysitting dilemmas, but they kept me connected to John's Fleet Street world. And George's attentiveness reassured me that one day someone who wasn't happily married to someone else would find me attractive.

Emboldened perhaps by the wine, one evening George asked me right out if I was thinking of killing myself. I responded that, of course, I was. Who wouldn't be? I promised that I wouldn't do anything while Hope was alive. But imminently each day I expected her to be struck down by a car or succumb to some fatal virus. It was surely only a matter of time.

George switched from wine to spirits. Whisky for him; strong, very strong, gin and tonic for me. 'We'll all be dead in a hundred years,' he reasoned. 'It's cheating to bale out before your allotted time.' As arguments for staying alive go, that sounded pathetic even to my distressed state of mind. I told him so. We bickered over it and parted.

He rang me up. He invited me over to his office after work. More gin and tonic. More bickering. Weeks passed. George was assiduous in ringing me up and bothering me on an almost daily basis. His arguments never really got much better. 'Your friends will miss you,' he'd say. Or: 'You won't know how things turn out for them.' To which I'd reply that I didn't care anyway and the only people I cared about in the world were dead except for Hope and that was all I could think about.

But gradually, gradually – like a string tugging a kite back to earth – his concern gently coaxed me back into the real world. There wasn't a moment when I thought: He's right, it is worth going on. It was more that his constant gentle nagging kept me anchored in the everyday rather than dreaming of oblivion.

When I think of all the people who have said to me since that they didn't write or call because they didn't know what to say and didn't want to make things worse, I want to say to them you should have done it anyway. Sometimes the most stupid, clunky, cringe-making comments are the ones that help the most because they bring you back to the here and now. No one should ever be afraid of saying the wrong thing. Saying nothing at all may turn out to be so much worse.

The feelings of wanting to kill myself may have faded but I was still on a downward spiral of depression. I couldn't sleep at night and couldn't get up in the morning. I had constant stomach cramps from tension and was drinking a lot on my own in the evenings. And smoking, too – more than a pack a day in my office at work and out in the garden at night in the belief that Hope wouldn't notice. She, meanwhile, was struggling at school. When she'd started in reception class just before Ellie got ill, Hope had been a bright child, able to write her own name, and on the point of learning to read and count. A year later she had regressed to the point where numbers and letters held no meaning for her. And she was short-tempered and demanding of attention in class. We were in a mess.

If we'd been left to our own devices, as I had been by

the hospital after John's death, then I don't know where we'd be. I thank God and the people who have contributed to funding Great Ormond Street that they have the resources to help. A nurse trained in bereavement counselling was assigned to visit us at home to keep an eye on us and she made it clear that we were welcome in the hospital and on the ward any time we wanted to drop by. It was after all mine and Ellie's home for eight months. I didn't want to go back but I asked for news of Ellie's friends: Bradley, Joe and Georgie Horlick. It wasn't good. One by one they had all died – all of her classmates were gone. Georgie was buried on what would have been Ellie's tenth birthday.

I did decide, however, to go back and visit the psychologist who had worked on the ward while we were in Great Ormond Street. I liked her no-nonsense approach and the fact that she had known both Ellie and myself. I made an appointment and took a long lunch break from work. I was looking forward to talking to her. Maybe someone who really understood, who really knew, could help my tortured brain. But as I started to walk down the road from the tube station there was a roaring sound in my ears. The white walls of the hospital appeared to me to be streaked with blood. They were running with blood. Ellie's blood. I was hallucinating – I knew I must be – but the images looked very real.

Sick and giddy and faint, I crouched in the gutter praying for the scenes to pass. They didn't. Somehow I managed to half crawl, half drag myself into the hospital foyer and croak to the girl on reception the name of the person I had come to see. I lay down on a bench and shut my eyes tight, trying to block out the terrible images and sounds, waiting for the psychologist to come and rescue me.

She got me up to her office but I was in a terrible state and clearly couldn't continue to come into the hospital for counselling. In fact, it was the last time I ever visited Great Ormond Street. To this day if I have to cross that part of London I give it a wide berth.

But I needed help badly. Could I pay, she asked hesitantly. Yes, I could pay. I don't know what would have happened if I couldn't. She gave me the name of a psychotherapist and told me to go and see her.

∞

At this point psychotherapists, psychiatrists, psychologists and counsellors were all very muddled up in my mind. Shockingly, when you think that I had been dangling over a mental health precipice for the past six years, most of what I knew came from Woody Allen films.

I now have the classifications more or less straight:

Counsellors help you cope with specific events and would be the first port of call for someone who is bereaved. The assumption is that you don't have any underlying mental health problems but need help getting through something very difficult and outside your experience. They don't delve deeply into your mind but simply aim to give you the tools to get through the tough times. The counsellor who had helped me after John's death would have been entirely appropriate, I expect, if it had not been for the complicating and largely misunderstood factor that I was giving birth to a posthumous child.

Psychiatrists are trained medical doctors with additional qualifications in mental health. They deal with the most severe kinds of mental illness and psychosis and can prescribe drugs if need be.

Psychologists are not medical doctors but have studied psychology to at least degree level, often beyond. They do not necessarily have any contact with patients, they may simply do research, although some operate as counsellors or psychotherapists, as well.

Psychotherapists are the ones you see in Woody Allen films. Theirs is the 'talking cure' invented by Freud, although since modified by many other practitioners, and the idea is to look back over your life to find reasons why you are finding it especially hard to cope with what are essentially normal life events such as bereavement.

It turned out I was going to see a psychotherapist and, inevitably, she was based in Hampstead. Also, inevitably, there was a couch to lie on although I preferred to perch nervously on the edge of a sofa. She wasn't a Freudian, she told me, which I thought a shame as that was the only kind of therapist I'd heard of. She was a Kleinian, which turned out to be quite similar, just a bit softer with a lot of emphasis on the inner child. In our first session I was prickly and difficult but prepared to give it a go, as I could hardly bear to carry on living feeling the way I did. So I was absolutely staggered when she said she would have to decide whether or not she was able to help me. This never happened in Woody Allen films. If I was paying surely it was her job to sit there and listen?

No, she said. If she didn't feel she could help me she wouldn't take me on. What did I hope to achieve out of therapy? A thousand answers crossed my mind. Relief from this pain. A reason for living? To bring John and Ellie back (I knew that couldn't happen but it was the only thing I really wanted). But the words that left my mouth amazed me: 'I want to be able to love again,' I said.

And I did. I knew by that stage I could carry on living. I didn't know whether I could ever risk my heart and love again.

She said she thought she could help me and outlined the terms. Sessions would last 50 minutes each – this is the world of the 50-minute hour. There would be no sessions in August or at Christmas or Easter. The rest of the time I would be expected to show up twice a week and if I missed a session I would still have to pay for it. No, I couldn't cancel even with 24 hours' notice. For her part she assured me that I could do or say whatever I felt or thought in the sessions. She would not take it personally. I did not have to impress her and whatever happened she would be there for me for as long as it took. This meant less than nothing to me. Nobody was there forever in my world.

So we began our sessions. Other than saying hello when she answered the door to me there were no greetings, no chit chat. She simply sat and waited for me to speak. Eventually, to break the silence, I would say the first thing that came into my head. She was always neutral in her responses. 'I see,' was the most frequent comment. Occasionally it was: 'So how does that make you feel?'

I hated the sessions and absolutely hated her. If I cried, she would wait impassive until I stopped. When I'd had 50 minutes, she'd say: 'Time's up', even if I was still crying, and I would stagger out into the street and go and sit in a coffee bar until I felt able to face the world again.

Often I'd skip sessions. But I still had to pay. And it added up to a lot of money, even on my salary. Usually I was late. Once or twice, before evening sessions, I would go to the wine bar for a drink first and turn up smelling of wine. There was not a flicker on her impassive face. I loathed the whole process. There had to be a better way. I went to my GP and asked for antidepressants. Again I encountered huge reluctance to give me anything I could harm myself with, but my distress was so evident, even in the surgery, that I managed to leave with a prescription for a very low dose of Seroxat, which works in roughly the same way as its more famous cousin Prozac.

Hallelujah. Ten days later I woke up in the morning having slept right through the night for the first time in – how long? Forever! The sun was shining. Actually, it wasn't. It was raining outside but I felt that the sun was shining. Intellectually, I knew that John and Ellie were dead but everything else felt okay. At last, I could cope. I carried on going to see my therapist, feeling a lot more cheerful about her. She was unimpressed and told me she was not in favour of drug treatment. Hmm! So much for impartiality. But I was coping so much better and sessions started to go so much better as well. Which was good, as everything else was going so much worse.

My father was clearly entering the last stages of his many battles against cancer and since he was now 69 we knew it was unlikely he'd survive this one. Each time he'd been diagnosed with a primary tumour apparently unrelated to the previous ones. Nobody could really tell us why lightning had struck four times. Maybe it was just bad luck. Or good luck that he'd survived this far. There was a theory that the aggressive radiation treatment he'd received in the Sixties for his testicular cancer was to blame but we never really knew.

At any rate the cancer was now in his stomach and it looked like time was running out. He had always been a difficult man – angry at the world. Largely, I always thought, because of his deprived upbringing in the East End of London before the war. But possibly, I now see, exacerbated by the fact that, as a man in early middle-age at the height of his powers, achieving the kind of success and status he could have only dreamed of as a child, he was constantly dogged by life-threatening illness.

Surgery to remove his stomach had left him fearful of choking and the chemotherapy he was on made him nauseous. He was also depressed. He should have died, not Ellie, he kept saying – as if there was any choice in the matter. He was at home; my mother couldn't leave the house even to go to the shops for food without arranging for someone to come in and sit with him.

He was offered a place at the Farleigh hospice in Chelmsford, about 20 miles away from where they lived, lucky to be offered it at all as the hospice movement is underfunded and not everyone who needs a place can get it. Should he take it up? My mother was run ragged caring for him but they both felt that when he went in he would never come out. Even with all my experience of death this was new territory to me, too. I saw that at least with John and Ellie there had been the distraction of trying to save them right up until the moment of death. To sit back and say aggressive treatment is no longer worth it, and that the end will not be far away, is unbelievably hard and my parents found it so.

It was a grim day when he became so fearful of his worsening condition, especially the choking feelings, that he said he would prefer to be in a hospice with full access to pain relief rather than at home. I went to visit him the next day with a feeling of dread and having decided that we would bring him home as soon as my mother had had a break and recovered her strength. So it was with some surprise that I found him sitting up in bed, in no pain, chatting to the nurses and sipping a whisky.

He spent just under a month in the hospice and it was a revelation to me that death, while terribly sad, need not be horrifying – especially not for someone who has had a chance to live their life fully. Although at not quite 70 – the biblical three score years and ten – my father could still be regarded as being short-changed, in my family that was starting to look long-lived.

The atmosphere in the hospice was always calm and bright. The nurses could take time to talk. The food was home-cooked – not that my father could eat it. Alcohol was allowed and, since he could still swallow, it made him feel more human to have a drink every evening. There were endless cups of tea and biscuits for visitors. I took Hope to visit him without a qualm. He was on a small ward with two other patients and at first I was shocked by this, thinking that someone who was dying would need privacy. I later regarded it as a plus – he had someone to talk to and take an interest in on the few occasions when the family weren't around. And the pain relief was superb. None of them was suffering – they were simply preparing.

Opposite my father was a young man with motor neurone disease. He was almost totally paralysed but he was chatty and good company and he loved his food. The nurses would bring him really delicious meals from the kitchen downstairs and sit flirtatiously by his bed to feed him.

My father had been fearful of death, so it was strange that acknowledging that he was close to death was like lifting a great stone weight from his shoulders. I believe he even started to enjoy the whole dying process. One evening when all the family were gathered around the bed, he told us he felt himself going. We all knelt down praying and crying as he told each of us how much he loved us and how much we had meant to him. He told me how proud he was of my achievement and how I'd worked to overcome the hand that life had dealt me. Then he got to his sister Jo, who was with us, too.

'Jo,' he said. 'I'm going. You've been a good sister to me.'

Pause.

'You were always such a slip of a girl . . .'

Opens his eyes and takes in her now matronly frame.

'But you're not any more, are you!'

Collapse of praying, weeping family into giggles as my father rallied – thoroughly enjoying the commotion he'd caused.

About a week later, he told us again that he thought he was going. Fr Anthony came and gave him the last rites. Again the family gathered around the bed, praying and crying.

'I'm going,' he said in a weak voice. 'I feel myself going back through time to the child I was before the war . . .'

Pause.

'Back and back . . . to before I was born.'

Long pause. Then he sat bolt upright in bed and said:

'Do you want to know the really interesting bit about the introduction of the Corn Laws?'

And, ever the barrister, lectured us all for 20 minutes on the origins of British law while we dried our tears, struggled to our feet and wondered whether he was having us on. Maybe he was going to carry on like this forever?

In fact, he slipped away one night while my mother was resting on the visitor's bed in the next room. After 44 years of marriage, she was devastated not to have been there with him at the end but the staff reassured her that patients often do die in the brief moments when their family are out of the room – as if only then can they bear to let go.

It was a good death and I am ever grateful to the hospice for making it so. But he was still my father and I was starting to feel that if I lost anyone else I would just curl up in a ball and die, too. Then only weeks after he'd died Jo, his sister – the one who'd been such a slip of a girl – collapsed with a stroke and never properly regained consciousness. She was not only my aunt but my godmother and greatest supporter. She was the one I'd turned to in the teenage years when – typically – I felt my parents didn't understand me. A trained nurse who'd helped set up the Macmillan cancer care service, she'd helped me negotiate the labyrinth of hospital services with both John and Ellie and then my father. Now she too was gone.

Hope took my father's death very hard as well. The eight months she'd spent living with her grandparents were the closest she'd come to having a father. We became creatures on the bottom of the seabed, below so many thousands of fathoms of sea water that no light could penetrate. In our dark, lonely world we could see nothing of the sky or the place we used to live. All we could do was lie there.

Chapter Eight

∞

THE LITTLE MERMAID

So is it worse to lose a child or a husband? The question is, of course, absurd. The death of anyone before their time is always terrible. Coming to terms with loss in whatever circumstances is always incredibly hard. The death of a partner brings practical difficulties and desperate loneliness but – without saying it's worse – there is something about the death of a child that sends you completely over the edge.

With every fibre of their being a parent will strive to protect their child. And if you can't it's as if the natural order of the universe has been overturned and then anything can happen. The sky might turn black or it could start raining frogs. You hear those stories of an eight stone mother lifting up a car to free a toddler trapped underneath. Or a father pushing a child out of the path of an oncoming lorry even if it means his certain death. And it makes sense. There are very few parents, I believe, who wouldn't give their life for their child. To be a parent is to want your child to survive even more than you want to do so yourself. If it were possible, I would have swapped places with Ellie in a heartbeat. And yet, I couldn't do anything. I couldn't save her. No one and nothing in the world could. My own impotence drove me mad.

For at least two years after her death, I would wake in the morning appalled at the thought of yet another day to be got through. Why was I alive? What was the point?

Why should I live when my child was dead? I would lie in bed as long as I could. If I'd been living entirely on my own I don't think I would have ever got up. But then Hope would wake and need her breakfast and the dogs would be barking so I'd stagger downstairs to face another day.

After Rosie – the dog John and I had bought – had died, I was without a dog for six months. But I couldn't bear the silence in the house. So I went out and found not one but two more dogs to take her place. The first one was a six-month-old Cavalier King Charles spaniel, named Georgie. He was partially deaf and totally un-house-trainable. I got him in the middle of winter when it was snowing. Each morning I would get up at about seven, go downstairs and clear up where he'd dirtied in the night. Then I would let him out into the garden. To encourage him to think that outside was good, I would sit with him on a bench, drinking my cup of tea. I remember it was a freezing winter; there was snow on the ground for some of the time but I didn't feel the cold. Nothing so mundane as ambient temperature made any impression on me. Georgie would gambol about, oblivious to anything I expected of him, then when we returned indoors, he would crap on the carpet.

I hardly minded at all. In fact, his uncomplicated approach to life was very welcome. So much so that when I saw an advert in the paper for a fluffy white Bichon Frise who needed re-homing because his owner couldn't cope, I added Sunny Jim to our household as well. He was cleaner about the house but very neurotic and would bark his head off at the slightest disturbance or chew all the fur off his paws if he was stressed. The two of them were little furry nightmares. If I didn't spring out of bed when I heard Sunny barking each morning they would poo all over the kitchen and chew up the furniture. Which would make me even more depressed than I would otherwise have been. But they were an incentive to get up and start the day.

It didn't occur to me that most single parents working full-time would have baulked at having three pets – because, of course, I had Hope's cat Alice as well. I liked the fact that they needed walking and feeding and letting in and out and thinking about. At night when Hope was asleep and I was alone, they would lie on my stomach in the long dark hours. For a great deal of the time they were my only company. I had become so difficult and bad tempered and my pain had gone on so long that even my most faithful friends found me hard going.

I was desperately lonely but I didn't miss John during this time. In fact, in a way, I was grateful that he wasn't around, that he'd died without knowing what more fate had in store for us. My own grief was so nearly too much to bear that I couldn't have coped with seeing his as well. In my time on the cancer wards I'd got to know enough couples to realise that the terminal illness and death of a child can smash up even the strongest relationship. You can see why. One half of the couple struggles to find a glimmer of hope and it coincides with the other crashing into despair. One's up when the other's down. They are never in synch. It was similar for me and Hope but because she was a child I had no expectation that she could support me. If John were alive, I know I would have expected him to make things better somehow and, of course, he wouldn't have been able to. Would our marriage have survived Ellie's death? I just don't know. So many couples split up under such pressures. My heart goes out to them.

I was a total mess and so was Hope. She struggled with reading and writing and even stopped growing for a full school year, going from being one of the tallest in the class to one of the smallest. It was as if the trauma had made every non-vital part of her system close down. She was just surviving, not thriving. Even her hair stopped growing, which was extra misery to her as she had short, tufty red hair which made her look like a boy when she wanted the long flowing locks she remembered her sister having before chemo.

Should I have stayed at home to look after her? I don't think so. If after John had died friends had wondered why I didn't give up on this work obsession of mine, they were convinced that this time, surely, I'd admit defeat. But I didn't. For a start my savings were quite meagre and wouldn't have lasted long. I had been earning a decent salary for three years but my childcare bills in that time had been horrendous so we couldn't have lived for long on what I'd saved. And even more importantly, I don't think Hope would have benefited from my constant presence. Although Natasha, our nanny, was desperately sad about Ellie's death she was naturally coping better than I was. Far better, I thought then and I think now, that Hope should be cared for after school by an upbeat loving nanny than come home to a mother who would certainly have gone round the twist stuck alone in a house all day with her grief.

My job was one of the few things linking me to the normal world. And thankfully, my career remained unscathed, even flourished. To be honest, I'm not quite sure how. When I look back on those times, I realise my mind was really very troubled. The only explanation I can offer is that in order to keep out the demons, I focused so intently on my work for the 10 hours that I managed to spend at the office each day that it was bound to have some result. And it did.

In the 12 months after Ellie's death, and despite the fact that my father was dying, I was named Editor of the Year for my work on *Prima*, and the new magazines I'd launched, *Prima Baby* and *Your Home*. And I was head-hunted by The National Magazine Company to become editor-in-chief of the hugely prestigious magazine *Good*

Housekeeping. This bothered my therapist who felt it was hardly the time for me to change jobs, but I didn't listen to her. Didn't she understand, my work was the only thing that was keeping me going?

∞

I was still going for therapy twice a week – when I didn't skip the sessions. I still hated it and it was costing me a fortune but on some level I knew that without it I'd be worse off. Gradually, very, very gradually, I had begun to accept that for 50 minutes twice a week I could sit on a sofa in her Hampstead living room and let out just how awful my life was and how dreadful I felt. There would be no judgement, no criticism, no exhortation to pull myself together. Just calm acceptance. And it's amazing how rare that is.

Friends might think they can offer that – and some very patient people can for a week or two. But month in, month out? After a time, even the most loving friend is inclined to snap and tell you to get over it. The trouble is that therapy is expensive and it takes ages to work. For the first two years I managed little in the way of proper therapy, the delving into why I felt quite so responsible for both John's and Ellie's deaths and so guilty at being left alive. Sometimes, often in fact, I would just sit and cry for most of the session. The rules were inflexible though. At the end of 50 minutes the therapist would say, not unkindly: 'Time's up.' And I'd shuffle out into the street clutching wads of tissue to my streaming nose and eyes.

It seemed at first a brutal system. As if she couldn't see or didn't care how distressed I was. But endless repetition finally dinned it into my brain that the point was that she was always, always there for me. My sessions were never cancelled nor did she ever run late and keep me waiting. When I couldn't depend on anything else – not even that those I loved would stay alive, I could at least depend on the fact that my therapist would be there for me. Clearly it was only by being strict about the time-keeping that she could guarantee that. To arrive and find the previous session had over-run or that she had been called away elsewhere would have been unendurable to me in my fragile state. But, even though she was utterly constant according to the terms she had laid out in our first session, it was to be years before I could really trust her enough to open up to her fully.

When I finally did so, we were able to explore together how it was that my overachieving, both at school and university, and subsequent glittering career, while fine in themselves, had served me badly when it came to coping with something I couldn't change. Like death. All my life, I'd tackled things that seemed hard and painful or even impossible with boundless energy and determination, usually to succeed. In the case of John's, then Ellie's death, I couldn't. No matter how hard I worked; no matter how much I tried nor what I endured, nothing could ever bring them back. The finality of death was inescapable and I was torturing myself more by trying to avoid it.

Much of my anguish was expressed at night. I had always been a poor sleeper – right from when I was a baby, as my mother would remind me. Now it was even worse. As sleep overwhelmed me, my defences would finally come down and my brain would be invaded by terrible nightmares. I had scabs on my palms from clench-ing my fists so tightly in my sleep that my nails dug in. They were my stigmata. The therapist encouraged me to keep a dream diary and talk about what happened in them. But to me, the trained scientist, dream analysis was roughly on a par with numerology or the Tarot – neither of which I believed in – and, in any case, once I started analysing the content of the nightmares, they mutated into formless night terrors where I would wake, sweaty and panting, not sure what had happened and what was real and what wasn't.

Obviously, I couldn't avoid sleep altogether but I tried to minimise it by sitting up late writing feverishly – although when I later read back what I'd written it often turned out to be gibberish. Or I would lie awake reading and re-reading bland, unchallenging books far into the night. My favourites were gentle country house detective novels from between the Wars. I particularly loved the Lord Peter Wimsey stories of Dorothy L. Sayers. I liked the lack of troublesome emotion and the triumph of cool logic over death.

∞

No wonder I was still on antidepressants. In October 2002, the current affairs programme *Panorama* broadcast an investigation into the advisability of prescribing some types of antidepressant, including Seroxat, the one I was on, to people with suicidal feelings. As I write now, nothing has been proven conclusively although Seroxat is no longer used to treat depression in under-18-year-olds but the thought of it gives me the chills. Could I, while under the influence of a drug, have abandoned Hope (that's hope with a lower case H, as well as my daughter)? I don't know. The fact is I didn't. The suicidal feelings had disappeared before I even started on the drugs and didn't return. Thank God. The drugs got me through the bit before the therapy started to work and for that I'm grateful. Knowing what I know now, would I have still have taken them? Almost certainly not. Although that answer might have been different had I not been able to afford the therapy. They were a help for a while but, need-less to say, they didn't, couldn't make everything all right again. Indeed, after the initial euphoria of being able to sleep through the night, they had turned out to be a mixed blessing.

On the plus side they entirely annihilated every sexual feeling in my body. I may have been lonely, very lonely, but I no longer craved sexual contact. I was no longer prone to sleeping with someone, anyone, just for the company, which had happened on a couple of occasions.

You'd think anyone with half a brain or an ounce of compassion would have seen I was in no fit state to pursue any sort of equal relationship, and steered well clear. But no. Clearly there are men out there for whom a woman in severe emotional distress is fair game. Possibly less scary to them than one who's able to make sensible judgements and spot their inadequacies. One, in particular, wooed me and courted me for weeks before I gave in to him. On a rational level, I knew it was hopeless and could never work out. But he was so attentive and flattering and apparently understanding, and I was so lonely that I allowed myself to trust him. For three and a half weeks it was heaven. Work and childcare meant we could only get together on a few sporadic occasions but when we could manage to see each other, he made me feel as if life was worth living again. Once he took me out for dinner but the attraction between us was so intense that we abandoned our meal in the middle of the starter and dashed back to his house to make love. When we were apart he sent me notes and gifts, and phoned endlessly.

Then one morning he rang, and told me he didn't think it was going to work out between us after all. He'd met someone else – a friend of mine actually – and he thought he'd rather give it a go with her. To him, I don't suppose it was anything at all. I was just a routine casualty of the dating game. But to me it was devastating. I was abandoned again. My battered mind couldn't distinguish between the overwhelmingly dreadful loss of John and Ellie and the essentially trivial pain of a putative relationship gone wrong. I felt I could trust no one. I closed down completely. The shell that had developed after John's death grew back and hardened over even more. No one would get through it ever again.

So the diminution of libido that is generally thought to be a negative side-effect of antidepressants was to me a bonus. I didn't want to get close to anyone and the drugs killed any rogue feelings that might have made it possible. More of a problem to me was that the drugs exacerbated the stress-induced stomach problems I'd suffered since Ellie's death. Now in addition to the cramps, I felt nauseous if I had more than one glass of wine. If I had more than two, I would get very hot and sweaty and then throw up. All the time I was working at *Prima* this was manageable. My job was mainly office-based and when I got home in the evening and wanted a drink, which I did every night, I coped by making sure I stuck to just the one and didn't drink on an empty stomach. Of course, my GP had told me not to drink while I was on antidepressants at all but, I reasoned, if I could get by without a drink then I wouldn't need the drugs anyway.

When I got the job at *Good Housekeeping* I was thrown into a much more sociable world. There were lunches with advertisers every day and glamorous cocktail parties most evenings. I would dutifully attend these functions but find myself tongue-tied when it came to making small talk. I would stand there amid all the swirling, laughing, chattering people, wanting to scream at them: 'Don't you realise my child has died. My husband died. Everyone is dying.'

Obviously I didn't do that so instead I would help myself to a glass of champagne from a passing waiter. On an empty stomach naturally. As the alcohol hit my bloodstream I would feel as if I could make a bit of small talk. Then, emboldened, I'd have another glass and another until I'd feel my temperature rising. Then I'd start to sweat and there'd be a pounding noise in my ears so I'd excuse myself and go to the ladies' toilet where I'd be sick.

Vomiting usually stopped the hot flushes but sometimes I had to lie down on the cool tiles of the cubicle to bring my temperature back down. Then I'd splash my face with cold water; brush my teeth with the toothbrush I learned to keep in my handbag and re-do my make-up. Sometimes I'd have sweated so much that I'd have to take off my top and dry it under the hand drier. But even so I'd only be gone around 10 minutes and, to be honest, I don't suppose anyone really noticed.

I didn't even mind very much myself. At least throwing up in the toilets was something to do and it was easier than answering the dreaded questions that are such a normal part of social intercourse such as: 'How many children do you have?' Or: 'Is your husband in this business, too?' They are such innocent questions but they caused me so much pain. Eventually, I got the hang of brushing off questions like that. Usually by mumbling then asking a question back. People always like to talk about themselves far more than they want to hear your answers. Now I'm recovered enough I know that I am not dishonouring John's and Ellie's memory by failing to make them part of inconsequential small talk.

But in those days I was far too raw to be able to say: 'Just one child.' Or: 'No, I don't have a partner at present.' To do so felt like denying their existence. So I would answer truthfully and it was always awful. It distressed me and killed the conversation. At cocktail parties people would move away from me. The dinner party I described ruining in the introduction to this book was just one of many. And I still tremble at the thought of one hideous taxi journey I endured. There was some sort of big football match on and the cab driver asked if I would be watching it.

'No.'

'Got kids? Will they be watching it?'

'One – she's not interested in football.' I was learning, at last. That would head the conversation off at the pass.

'Your husband though – bet he'll watch it.'

'He's er . . . He's er . . . He's not around.'

The driver stopped at the lights and turned round to face me. 'Well, he ought to take an interest for the kiddie's sake. It's hard for kids at school these days if they don't know about football.'

It was raining and I was miles from my destination but I opened the taxi door and stumbled out into the street, stuffing a £5 note in through the driver's window. Okay, now I was wet and lost but at least I didn't have to answer any more questions.

I eventually stopped wearing my engagement ring for the same sorts of reasons. I'd taken off my wedding ring after John died when my fingers swelled during pregnancy. It had never fitted very well anyway. But when the puffiness went down, I put the diamond ring he had given me, which had previously been his mother's, back on the third finger of my left hand. Then, one day, an acquaintance, whom I hadn't seen for ages, grabbed my hand and shrieked: 'Wonderful, you're engaged. Who is he?' This was seven years after John's death so her assumption was quite reasonable – to anyone but me, of course.

All social interaction was laced with these pitfalls. It was to be years before I managed to deflect questions about my family status gracefully and without getting upset. And it made the corporate entertaining that went with my new job a minefield.

The only person I told about the problem was June, who'd come with me from *Prima* to *Good Housekeeping* as deputy editor. She accompanied me to functions as often as she could and would hover nearby ready to leap in and change the subject if it got too tricky. She would even hold my head while I vomited in the toilets then help me freshen up again. Together, we got through the social round which was a necessary part of the job. And it was worth it because I adored working on *Good Housekeeping*. It was truly my dream to be editing a glossy magazine yet one with the scope to showcase top-class writing and fund proper investigations through the Good Housekeeping Institute. I had a large staff of really intelligent, thoughtful journalists – all experts in their field – and the support of both a fantastic publisher in Simon Kippin, who later launched the highly successful magazine *Glamour*, and a brilliant Barnum of a boss in Terry Mansfield. I'd been for my first interviews with Terry as my father lay dying. He was only a little younger than Dad and like him had grown up in the East End of London, leaving school without any qualifications and reaching the top of his trade by sheer hard graft. They even looked alike. Although for business reasons Terry and I would have the most frightening clashes, he became over time very much a mentor to me. And a year after hiring me he went ahead and bought up the entire UK operation of the company I'd previously worked for, absorbing the titles *Best* and *Prima* along with my own creations *Prima Baby* and *Your Home* into the National Magazines portfolio, although I remained working exclusively on *Good Housekeeping*. Professionally, I was happier than at any other time in my life. The extent to which I had to override my misery to take advantage of these wonderful opportunities was, to my way of thinking, just the price I had to pay. And so I became The Little Mermaid in the fairy story, whose dream of living on dry land was paid for by losing her voice and every step she took felt like treading on knives. As a child I wondered why she didn't just go back to living under the sea. What was so great about dry land? Now I knew.

I was rendered almost dumb in most conversation by my grief. And even to get through the most mundane day was like treading on knives. But, despite the pain, I knew

I could not go back to life on the seabed. I had to live and breathe the air.

And what rarefied air I was breathing. *Good Housekeeping* really was the most fantastic, entertaining stimulating place to be. Within six months of taking over, I'd pushed its circulation up, overtaking everything else in its market and becoming the market leader. With its heritage and fame I could ring up anyone I liked and ask them to write for me. Women I'd long admired – Shirley Conran; Glenys Kinnock; Margaret Jay; Susan Greenfield – all obliged. I was even becoming a little bit famous myself.

The renewed success of *Good Housekeeping* and my status of Editor of the Year combined with my recent tragic history made good copy for newspapers. Of course, I was flattered to be asked to describe how I was reinventing such a venerable magazine. And I didn't mind being asked to talk about John and Ellie. What upset me at parties and dinners was being expected to pretend they had never existed. I was always completely comfortable with talking about them directly, not only because it helped to bang the drum for charities like the Leukaemia Research Fund and the Anthony Nolan Trust but, more personally, because I wanted to keep them alive in people's minds and not let them be forgotten.

A few interviews appeared in a couple of newspapers and trade magazines. Most were straightforward. In one or two, the writers rather over-egged the Downing Street connection, which was predictable really and not of my doing. But one article was downright nasty, suggesting I should shut up and get back home to my remaining child rather than parading my pain in public. When I read the piece, it was like being punched. It knocked the air out of me. This woman who'd interviewed me appeared quite nice to my face yet she portrayed me as fat, zombie-like and so desperate for attention that I would use the deaths of my husband and child to get it. I was staggered. What on earth was going on in her mind that she felt so threatened by me?

I was shocked and embarrassed that people should read such descriptions of me but even so I wasn't deeply hurt. It reminded me again that some people are so afraid of death that they will lash out if forced to confront it.

Much more painful were the reactions of some of my friends. I had, I can see now, become a total nightmare to them. It had been so long since I had been cheerful, or pleasant, or had the energy to be interested in their lives. And even when I did rally and summon up interest again, it all sounded so silly. It wasn't that I didn't want to hear them complaining about how all the kids had gone down with chicken pox or that a husband was paying too much attention to a glamorous younger woman at work. It was just that such troubles were on a different scale from what I'd been through. And if I did manage to express an interest (and to be fair I didn't always), it didn't really sound convincing. So in the end nobody bothered telling me about what was happening to them. And, gradually, I was losing the narrative thread of my friends' lives.

That's the thing about loss. It doesn't stop with the death: the losses just go on multiplying. And then there was another big row.

As I've said before, death always brings on a fight and undertakers should warn mourners about it. But the truth is that however much you know that it's going to happen, you still can't stop it. And, of course, you've got a lot to be angry about. Angry as hell that this person you love so much has left you and caused you such unendurable pain. But you can't be cross with them because they suffered so much and they didn't want to die, so you've got all this rage sloshing around inside you and, boy, is it going to come out. But how? Where?

The row with my mother after John's death had upset me so much, I had been determined never to let such a thing happen again. I managed to get through Ellie's death and funeral, only falling out with one person, A priest as it happens, and I reckon they are – or should be – professional about death and take it on the chin, as it were, so it wasn't too awful. I thought I'd got away with it. But I was to discover that if you don't get it all out of your system at the funeral then the next best thing is the anniversary.

It was almost exactly a year after Ellie's death when a very close friend rang up and bawled me out for all my bad behaviour. She said I wasn't interested in her or her life. I was taking for granted all the help and consideration she'd given me over the years. But she was a person, too, and had feelings. She went on and on. I forget what else she said but it was almost certainly all true. At first I was stunned. Then I tried to pacify her to calm her down, to explain that I knew I'd been a pain but I was doing the best I could. Then I lost my temper. Big mistake. It was as if the funeral row, which I'd managed to avoid, had been building inside me for a year . . .

As it happened, I was spending that weekend down in the Devon countryside where the reception on my mobile phone was patchy at best. As I let rip, the phone cut out. Or she hung up. So I fumed and paced about until I got a signal then I called and ranted again. And again. And again. The gist of my argument was that I may well have been a pain and selfish and inconsiderate, but no one whose children were alive and well had any right to criticise me. It's not wrong as arguments go but I was failing to take into account the terrible toll that my sufferings had also taken on my friends, who got no kudos or thanks for their constancy – nor any hope of getting anything back in return. Nor even any hope of an end in sight.

But I didn't see that then. I couldn't. I was so angry. I never found out what was going on in my friend's life that she felt the loss of my support so keenly that week-end. Maybe it was just the culmination of so much stuff over the year that she couldn't ever see a time when I would look after her instead of the other way round. So she had a go at me and I had a go right back at her.

We never spoke of the row again yet it took months to undo the damage. No, make that years. In fact, I'm not really sure if it's right yet. Or will ever be.

I was learning that there is no part – not one tiny frag-ment – of your life that death leaves unchanged. Nothing you can take for granted as being the same. Everything was falling apart around my ears. The only thing that gave me any pleasure, which conformed to the known rules of the universe, was my job. And that was a double-edged sword. I would have given anything to be able to run away from everything that was so painful in my life – to move to another country and not see or speak to anyone – but perversely it was my job that was making me stay and face it. Then the opportunity for a partial escape came as a direct result of my father's death.

∞

Despite coming such a long way since his humble begin-nings in the East End of London, and although barristers are reputed to be wealthy, my father hadn't been that well-off when he died. He did, however, leave each of his children a small sum of money. I decided to use mine as the deposit for a weekend cottage.

The logic behind this was that my mother had quickly

sold the house they lived in, the one where I grew up, and despite having my home in London I was feeling rootless. Every other weekend for much of my adult life I had returned to our family home. It was a beautiful house and even though I'd officially moved out and married two decades earlier, I still kept all my childhood stuff there. It hadn't been a problem as there was plenty of room. But as my mother struggled with the upkeep of this huge uneconomic house and the formal gardens throughout my father's final illness, she had stopped taking pleasure in it and come to regard it as a millstone around her neck. Within three months of his death, she had sold it, disposed of most of the contents and moved into a small, easy-to-maintain bungalow nearby. People say you shouldn't move house within a year of bereavement and, broadly speaking, I think that's good advice. But people have to do what they have to do. For her it was a relief. For me it was yet more minor losses to add to the bigger ones.

So I found a tiny town house three miles down the road from the village where my mother lived and where I'd grown up. It wasn't a country cottage in the conventional sense. It had been built in the Seventies and was just off the main road, so it was handy for the shops, and even the railway station. But it had a balcony from which you could see the river. And it contained no memories.

The house in London was full of John's stuff and Ellie's stuff. I had wanted to move away for ages but it was never the right time. No sooner was I back on my feet after John's death than Ellie became ill. Now, I was scared to move in case I lost track of some of those memories. The three little steps that led down from the hall to the kitchen where Ellie had learned to climb stairs. One of her dirty hand prints on the white wall of the living room that I'd never had the heart to wash off. The chair positioned in front of the TV and next to the phone where I'd been trapped day after day, night after night, breastfeeding her when she was colicky. I wanted to escape but I couldn't bear to leave. The house in Burnham represented the perfect compromise.

It was very cheap and very shabby. With my brothers' help I found a local builder who would gut it for me, but I had very little money to spend on renovations so my mother and I did a lot of the unskilled work ourselves. All that autumn we heaved manky, soiled carpets and strips of old wallpaper into the back of the Volvo I'd borrowed from work and deposited them at the municipal dump. Then we'd drive up the A13 to IKEA and buy cheap flatpacked furniture to furnish my little doll's house, often returning with Hope perched on top of the purchases that filled the car. After a full week at work it was hard labour but I was like a woman possessed. At last the opportunity to create something rather than see it destroyed.

We made a curious working party – two widows of different generations and a small, profoundly bereaved child – but we tackled jobs that were way beyond our strength and capabilities. Once I managed to force a five-seater sofa, that I'd snapped up on special offer, in the back of the car and drive it back to my mother's house where we hauled it alone into the garage for safekeeping until we could find a team of strong men to get it into my house. It took the best part of six months to do up the house but finally it was liveable. I bought a tiny pony for Hope to ride so she had something to do on Saturdays and Sundays (yet another animal to care for!) but mostly we just rested and recuperated and tried to rebuild our battered hearts.

We took to spending every weekend there, which relieved our beleaguered circle of friends from what had become by now the onerous duty of getting us through the days I wasn't occupied at work and Hope didn't have school. Yet we were both happy to spend the days on our own or with just my mother, or my brother Hugh and his family for company. We re-trenched and huddled down into ourselves.

On Saturdays I would shop and cook and clean with the kind of loving attention to detail that I'd never exhibited in London. The routine repetitive tasks were very consoling in themselves. Afterwards I'd take Hope to ride Rose the pony and then we would go to church in the evening. For Catholics a Saturday evening service counts the same as a Sunday morning one. The parish priest was impossibly old and frail and not of the modern, analytical school of religion. In his simple 10-minute sermons, he preached only love and acceptance and forgiveness. There was nothing I could argue with, nothing I could take issue with. I would simply sit and let his wise, gentle words wash over me. Hope and I would take communion along with the rest of the tiny congregation and then every week we sang the same hymn, *For Those In Peril On The Sea*, in recognition of the fact that this was a fishing and sailing community.

On Sundays Hope would ride again in the morning and then in the afternoon we would take the dogs for long, long walks along the sea wall, bracing ourselves against the icy wind from the North Sea. The landscape in that part of Essex is mostly reclaimed marshland and very flat indeed. It is not generally believed an area of great natural beauty but it is wild and free and the sky is huge. It's where I grew up and it's home to me. I suppose we always gain strength from the place we call home.

During one of our quiet and lonely weekends there I threw away the remains of my antidepressants and decided to allow my mind to feel whatever it needed to feel. Finally, and very slowly, I began to heal.

Chapter Nine

∽

THE LONG CRAWL BACK

By the start of 2002, three and a half years after Ellie's death, I had long since given up any expectation that therapy – or indeed anything else – could cure my deep unending heartache. It was enough for me that I wasn't on antidepressants any more and I had found a way of living that was bearable. Weekdays working. Weekends spent with Hope at our house in Burnham. That was all I needed for survival. And, most of the time, to be surviving at all seemed remarkable.

So initially I didn't recognise the signs that something was changing within me. The nightmares started almost imperceptibly to diminish and I began to sleep through the night. At first, I thought it was a fluke. I'd been an insomniac long before what I referred to as the 'bad stuff' had started happening. But eventually I realised, yes, it was definitely happening.

My bedtime rituals of reading and diary writing, which I used to stave off the moment when sleep overtook me, gradually lessened and then were abandoned altogether. I would sleep deeply, only coming to, with a start, at 7am as if I'd forgotten to do something. That something being waking at four and tossing and turning for hours. I still had nightmares but not every night. And they had changed. Where they had been anguished pleas from John and Ellie to save them, now they were less frightening; merely frustrating. I dreamed I was constantly on the move, trying to catch an aeroplane or a train but being thwarted at every turn by lost luggage or delayed flights. It was as if my mind was battling my attempts to move on. Surely there was still more packing or unpacking to do?

Even so, for the first time in my life, sleep became good. It was a desirable activity. And I could do it. I set about sleeping at every available opportunity. Hope's regular bedtime was still 9pm. As soon as she'd gone up I would let the dogs out in the garden for 10 minutes, prepare everything I needed for the morning then follow her up. On weeknights, I aimed for a good nine hours – easily five hours per night more than I'd been getting previously. At weekends, without school or work to get up for, I'd go for the full 12, with ideally a couple of hours on both Saturday and Sunday afternoons on the sofa, while Hope watched a video.

Deep, glorious, blissful sleep. I moved over into the centre of the bed for the first time since John's death and slept languorously, spread-eagled, among a pile of pillows. I had a vague feeling of resentment that by this time I'd done years in therapy and I was – as I saw it – no more over Ellie's death than I had been before. After all it wasn't as if I'd sought out therapy for my sleep problems. But I didn't care. My new-found interest in sleeping was compensation enough and I had a lifetime to catch up on.

As my body became properly rested, the stomach problems that had plagued me since Ellie's death disappeared and my appetite returned. With a vengeance.

I didn't give food much thought when I was growing up and we didn't have a lot of money for treats and meals out. Food was fuel – as simple as that. There were few convenience foods available then and my mother had little interest in or spare time for preparing elaborate recipes from scratch. She served up plain food in large enough quantities to satisfy her family's huge appetites. We never had the luxury of being fussy eaters. At mealtimes, my brothers and I would wolf down everything in sight in the certain knowledge that there would be nothing else until the next meal. No biscuits or crisps or sweets. As a teenager I was Kate Moss skinny, or possibly even thinner. Even in my twenties and thirties, size 10 clothes hung off my 5' 9" frame, making me the envy of friends who struggled with their weight. My beanpole shape meant that I could dress extremely well on very little money, as even cheap clothes look good if you're tall and slender. I put on some weight after each of the children was born but not much. I was still indifferent to food and when I was busy would skip meals altogether. For my fortieth birthday my then boss enquired of friends where he could take me for a really special meal to celebrate. And got the answer from my colleagues: 'Anywhere will do, she's not really that interested in what she eats.'

Five years later it was a very different story: the reawakening of my appetite combined with working next door to the extensively equipped kitchens of the Good Housekeeping Institute. The cookery editor, Felicity Barnum-Bobb, had worked with me before on *Prima* but my appreciation of her efforts had until then been purely journalistic as our offices had been so small she had to do all her cooking off-site. Now, all day, every day, wonderful smells would waft out of the kitchens and she and her team triple tested every single one of the recipes that went into the magazine. And most of the staff, unlike me, were absolutely passionate about food, talking about it constantly, many of them – and not just those who were employed in the food department – being very accomplished cooks.

Aggie MacKenzie was one. She had been an assistant editor mainly working on rewriting copy when I joined the magazine. But I was so impressed by her foodie credentials that I put her in charge of the Good Housekeeping

Institute. Not such a clever management move on my part as it turned out, because it was from there that she was snapped up to co-present the series *How Clean Is Your House?* so we ended up losing her from the magazine to TV stardom. But in the interim we had the benefit of her passionate interest in food.

If I called a lunchtime meeting we always ate whatever menus were being tested in the Institute kitchens. And hardly an afternoon meeting passed without someone producing a cake or dessert recipe they'd been experimenting with at home. Aggie always made all her own bread, which she would bring into the office. And even when we went away to stay in a rented country house for an editorial conference she lugged her heavy Kitchen Aid mixer with her and not only made scones for tea but then got up halfway through dinner, and tottered in high heels, several glasses of wine the worse for wear, out into the kitchen, and mixed up some dough, putting it to rise overnight so we would have fresh bread for breakfast in the morning.

Through Aggie and the cookery department I got to meet famous cooks and chefs whose approach to food couldn't have been more different from what I'd grown up with. Cooking had moved away from the complicated sub-cordon bleu recipes popularised during my childhood by Fanny Craddock and which my mother had found too fussy and complicated. Now it was all about using the freshest and best ingredients, cooked as simply as possible. Aggie would report back to me first and then in the magazine on what the latest food trends were. Where to get the best cheese or really delicious cold meats from a tiny Italian deli in Soho. She disdained the use of margarine and anything artificial. In fact, once when in a feeble attempt to keep up with the staff I made a chocolate cake and brought it into the office, she practically spat it out when she realised I'd used what she liked to refer to as 'ersatz' ingredients. However, she finally convinced me that even if you worked full-time and had kids, as she did, it was still possible to prepare fresh, healthy food every night.

Inspired by Aggie and armed with Felicity's very-easy-to-follow recipes, which I would eagerly run off from my computer rather than waiting for them to appear in print, I would go home at weekends and experiment. There were two good farm shops near my house in Burnham and I quickly discovered the difference between organic, free-range produce and the mass-produced stuff I had been buying. Every weekend I bought mountains of seasonal vegetables for fresh soups and soon wondered why anyone would resort to a packet or a tin when it was so cheap and easy to make yourself.

On Saturday nights while we were at church I would leave an organic chicken casserole or Irish Stew simmering away in the oven for our return. I baked apples and stewed gooseberries to serve with cream afterwards. Our quiet evenings in the country turned into gastronomic experiments. Even when we got back to London late on Sunday evenings I would position Hope by the cooker stirring a wild mushroom risotto while I unpacked our bags. Thanks to all our travelling Hope had never been a picky child and cooking was something she loved to do with me. We both found it very therapeutic.

My new-found interest in food also helped me cope with business lunches. Before regaining – or should that be gaining – an appetite, I'd been indifferent to the amazing array of world-class restaurants I'd been treated to in the course of my work. Now I would look forward to the fishcakes at the Ivy; the soufflé served only downstairs at Langans and the steak tartare at the Caprice. I hoped for invitations to eat seafood at Sheekey's or roast beef with all the trimmings at the Savoy Grill. And with my interest in food came a new-found confidence in small talk. No longer did anyone have to plug away at conversation with me, veering uncertainly towards dangerous territory such as family life. I was becoming knowledgeable, even expert on food. I could talk with authority on the origins of certain ingredients and short cuts to preparing gourmet meals at home.

The only problem was that I was getting fatter.

My size 12 suits were too tight, so I bought 14s, then 16s when they got too tight as well. Above size 16 it's quite hard to find tailored clothes but the joy of working on a magazine is the multiplicity of shopping choices you discover. So I switched to the pleated designs of Issey Miyake which are infinitely expandable and I loved the loose flowing garments from the Ghost label, teamed with soft cashmere wraps in jewel colours. Despite my size, the fact that I was earning quite a lot of money by now meant I was better dressed than ever before. I treated myself to a long coat in a silk tweed with a deep fake fur collar by the avant garde designer Yohji Yamamoto. It swept the floor, swirling about in a most satisfactory way, and I wore it whenever I needed to impress, which was often. To anyone who didn't know me I probably looked very glamorous, if a little on the large side. But I hated myself. When I looked in the mirror a stranger with a puffy face looked out. I loathed appearing on TV, which I had to do occasionally, because of having to see myself on the monitor. I didn't look like my mental image of myself.

I wanted to be me again. I didn't want to be this plump, sleepy person that tragedy had produced. But I had no idea how to find my true self among all the protective rolls of fat. Even though I worked in a business where diets were the stock in trade, I reached the age of 45 without ever having been on one. Back in my days as a radical beauty editor I'd written an article on the then new theories based around the book *Fat Is A Feminist Issue* by Susie Orbach. It had made a deep impression on me and ever since I'd believed diets were evil. Not unreasonable since, in the past, I'd always eaten anything that came my way and never gained weight. For most of my life my diet had largely consisted of cheese sandwiches, or – if I felt like cooking – cheese on toast, with fruit for the vitamins and a couple of bars of chocolate daily. Now, I was eating proper meals on a regular basis and it was all good, healthy stuff, or so I thought. So why wasn't I getting fitter and slimmer? What was going wrong?

∞

During Ellie's illness, Cherie had introduced me to the beauty therapist Bharti Vyas. Bharti is a controversial figure in some ways but she is also, I believe, extremely gifted not merely as a beautician but as a healer. The first time I visited her she took me in her arms and said: 'You look after your daughters, I will look after you.'

She was as good as her word although I was less good about making time to go and see her. But when I could fit it in, which wasn't often, I would run round to her salon in Chiltern Street where she would massage me and rub oil in my hair and then wrap me in warm blankets, put her famous compression boots on my legs, which rhythmically inflated and deflated, drawing out puffiness, and I would drift off into a deeply relaxed state for half an hour. Then I would jump into her tiny shower to get rid of the pungent smells of the ayurvedic herbs she used, and then dash back to work.

It was Bharti who first broached the subject of my weight. With her combination of motherliness and bossiness she told me I'd feel and look much better if I simply cut out wheat and dairy for a month. So no more cheese sandwiches but also no milk in my tea, no cheese, no yoghurt, no bread, no pasta, no cakes. I lost about a stone very rapidly and felt elated. But then the weight loss stopped. I should have listened to Bharti and let my body adjust to the new regime, but I was elated to be feeling this good at last and anxious to lose more weight. I booked up an appointment with another famous natural therapist, the nutritionist who'd got actress Kate Winslet to drop four stones by apparently 'reading' her face and telling her what foods to avoid.

She was tiny and chic and much more alternative than I'd bargained for. Her opening remarks were: 'Well, I know why you've come here – to lose all that fat!' She called me fat at least 10 times in the course of an hour and squidged my tummy several times. She looked at my face, my skin, my eyes, my hairline and scalp. She checked my nails, weighed me, measured me, then wrote a prescription for vitamins and handed me a sheet of paper outlining a strict detox diet. If I followed it to the letter, she said, I would lose a stone and a half in three weeks. I would then return and she would tell me what I could eat to stay that weight for the rest of my life.

It sounded wonderful. I took the prescription to a pharmacy and bought all the vitamins and herbal supplements I needed, which came to over £50, and, having made such a huge investment, decided to start the diet immediately. I was allowed a baked potato and raw veg for lunch and felt fine. By 3.30pm I started to fancy my regular afternoon Diet Coke – badly! At that point I was downing several cans of Coke and cups of strong coffee daily in order to overcome the constant sleepiness I felt. But caffeine was banned. By 5pm I had a really bad headache and was hallucinating about Coke and Starbucks coffee. That evening I went to a networking party for women journalists but could drink only water – quite a departure for me as I would usually have five or six glasses of wine at these evening events. My headache turned into an agonising starburst over my left eye.

Virtually every known foodstuff was banned on the

diet except potatoes, which I hate. I could have unlimited green vegetables and one piece of boiled fish or chicken per day. Breakfast was interesting . . . The night before you had to mix up a cup of oats with water and bake in the oven for half an hour to form a sort of soggy oatcake. In the morning I would eat it with a scrape of butter and sliced cucumber. It certainly put me off food until lunchtime. Not only were tea, coffee and Coke banned but I wasn't allowed any snacks – no fruit, no sweets, no bread, no milk, and no alcohol. I especially missed the fruit. The nearest thing I was allowed was just half a tomato a day.

By Day 3, I was so nauseous from the shock to my system that I had to rearrange all my business entertaining for the weeks ahead as I couldn't bear to be around food or drink. Even a weak cup of mint tea upset me now. All I could do was sip mineral water.

I was clearly too fragile for such extreme measures and fell off the wagon on Day 5 when I spotted a (totally forbidden) banana on June's desk and guzzled it down, followed by some cakes from the kitchen and a cup of milky coffee. Even though I know many people who have lost weight and improved their health by detoxing, and despite the fact that I actually came to quite like the soggy oatcakes – and still occasionally make one for my breakfast, I couldn't stick to the diet. It was too severe for me in my still fragile state and involved too many potatoes which I have always mentally referred to as 'poisonous tubers'. At school we used to be made to clear our plates but I couldn't force down the potatoes so I'd hide them in the pocket of my uniform and then throw them in the lake in the grounds when no one was looking.

∞

Back to the drawing board. I asked around discreetly among friends and colleagues who seemed to know about weight control and was told to try WeightWatchers. I was amazed. Slimming clubs were the anti-Christ for those who'd imbibed the law that diets made you fat. But by this time I didn't care. So much of what I'd previously believed about life had turned out to be untrue anyway; this was yet one more thing. I found a Friday evening class near home, took my courage in both hands and enrolled. To my embarrassment I discovered that I knew at least half the other people in the class, including those who I'd always thought of as naturally slim. But by now my researches were telling me that the slim people are the ones who exert an iron discipline over their weight, even if they claim to be able to eat what they like. The fact that I'd got away without bothering for so long was actually my good luck, which was a useful reminder to me that I hadn't been unfortunate in *every* area of my life.

The WeightWatchers diet is very straightforward. You count points, which are essentially calories but adjusted for saturated fat content to encourage you to choose healthier foods. You can eat what you like – just not very much of it. I was allowed 20 points a day which worked out at about 1,400 calories. It's easy to go over so you have to write down every single thing you eat. Doing so was a revelation.

No wonder I was putting on weight despite eating healthier food than ever before. I was eating it as well as, rather than instead of, the old unhealthy stuff – and in frightening quantities. In my loneliness food had gone from being simply fuel to being my friend and comforter. Just as you should never drink alone because your idea of what's a reasonable amount flies out the window, I discovered that eating alone was also perilous. I had thought nothing of scoffing a whole packet of biscuits – more than a day's allowance of calories – as I watched TV in the evening. Cooking for just Hope and myself would mean a roast chicken for two. And why not wash it down with a bottle of wine, then finish up with dessert? Luckily Hope still had that inner voice that told her to stop eating when she was full, so she hadn't got fat as well. But now at last, I could see where my problems lay. I was eating my feelings, as the teenage kids like to say.

And drinking them.

I loathe beer and spirits. I was never drunk and rarely had a hangover but I was still putting away a sizeable quantity of wine each week – way in excess of the acceptable amount for a woman. I had become so used to downing a bottle of wine a day that I wasn't even feeling the effects. Or so I thought. The only way to get by on 20 WeightWatcher points a day was to cut right back on alcohol. Even half a bottle was four whole points – the same as a breakfast or a light meal. I stopped drinking at lunchtime, at weekends and on my own in the evening, allowing myself just a glass or two if I was socialising midweek. It was hard to go back to making small talk without the tongue-loosening effect of wine, but nowhere near as hard as giving up caffeine had been when I was on the detox diet, so I stuck with it.

The weighing-in at WeightWatchers is confidential but I found it utterly, utterly humiliating to have to get on the scales each week. Margaret, the meeting leader, was unfailingly positive and encouraging. Once when I gained two pounds in a week, she clucked supportively: 'It gives you gyp, doesn't it – but you wait, you'll have lost double next week.' And I did, spurred by the thought that if I didn't I'd have to keep revisiting this hell for longer. I was hungry every day for five months but at the end of it I had lost 22 pounds – the remainder of the weight I'd put on during the dark days. My face, which had become an oval blur, popped back into focus. My clothes hung off me so I bought new suits by Armani with nipped-in waists and tailoring. The few people who could remember what

I looked like before my life took its downward turn said it was like having the old Lindsay back.

But just losing weight wasn't enough. I was desperately unfit and even though I'd finally managed to quit smoking on New Year's Eve 2001, I was still wheezy and out of breath. In order to speed my progress in getting back in shape I decided to join a gym near the office. Sensibly they insisted on giving me a full health check before letting me near the equipment and that too was a nasty shock. I had curvature of the spine, which was giving me constant back pain, no muscle tone, pathetic lung capacity and hardly any cardiovascular endurance. At one point the physical training instructor examining me couldn't even detect one particular muscle at all. She called over a colleague and they both searched for it. Was I deformed? Had I been born without the full complement of muscles? 'No, here it is,' he said. 'It's just a flicker but it's there!' Physically I was a wreck.

It hadn't always been that way. At school and university I had been a top-class fencer, captaining the East of England Ladies' Team. Although I'd stopped fencing competitively when my career took off, I'd always taken dance classes, swum and run just for the pure pleasure of it. I'd taken what my body could do for granted. Now it seemed brutally unfair to me that my reward for a decade spent grieving and caring for my family should be to end up overweight, unfit and old before my time. It was as if on top of everything else I'd been required to sacrifice my youth, my health and my looks.

I was far too enfeebled to work out in the gym, and even swimming, which is supposed to be very safe if you are unfit, made my already crocked back feel even worse. Eventually I found a gentle yoga class taught by a very sweet young girl who would encourage her pupils to spend a good 20 minutes of each session lying down wrapped in warm towels scented with lavender oil. It was very soothing and often I dropped right off to sleep. It hardly seemed like exercise at all but the gentle movements began to reawaken my dormant body.

Eventually, I felt strong enough to progress on to Pilates, which I'd first studied 20 years previously in my beauty editor days. It's a series of very slow controlled movements that isolate and strengthen various muscles. It was recommended to me by the osteopath whom I'd consulted about my back problems. For the first three months I hated it − it was like trying to pat your head and rub your tummy at the same time. But I persevered − after all I was used to slogging on through situations I hated − and eventually got the hang of it. Gradually my shoulders straightened and my back lengthened, my posture improved, and eventually I undid enough of the damage wreaked on my body to be able to start jogging, working out with weights and getting properly fit.

What with the gym membership and the cost of classes, it wasn't cheap trying to regain a physicality I'd previously taken for granted. But the cost in terms of time was even greater: evenings I could have spent with Hope, lunchtimes I could have been catching up on work, shopping or seeing friends. I discovered it takes a certain degree of selfishness to be healthy. You have to put yourself first on a daily basis but I had long ago lost the knack of doing that. For years there had always been someone's needs greater than mine. When you are caring for someone who is very sick or mourning their death, well-meaning friends will tell you to look after yourself. To take some exercise, to eat healthily. 'You're no good to anyone if you let yourself go,' they always say. I've said it myself. I even quote that bit they tell you in safety demonstrations on aeroplanes. You know that bit about fitting your own oxygen mask before attempting to help those who depend on you.

I wish now that through the bad days I had been able

to hold on to my sense of self a bit more. But I don't know many people who can. Being so wrapped up in someone else's fight for existence necessitates switching off many of your feelings about yourself. I think possibly that when a pride in your appearance and interest in your own health starts to reappear that maybe means you are on the mend. It did for me anyway.

To someone who hasn't been through it, this fretting about weight loss and muscle tone might seem incredibly trivial, when John and Ellie had lost their lives altogether. But I have come to realise that it's common in the bereaved state to neglect yourself so much that it might almost be called a passive form of suicide. I don't know that my drinking and smoking, combined with my unhealthy eating habits, would have killed me any time soon. But I do know they would have shortened my life eventually. And there was a time when that thought pleased me. So much of recovering from bereavement is about deciding to live rather than hoping to join the people you've lost.

I didn't know the television presenter Paula Yates personally, although we did have some friends in common, and I was very much saddened by her death in 2000 from a drug overdose. It seemed to me, watching from afar, that she lost the ability to care for herself after her partner Michael Hutchence's death three years before. And that I could understand. While illegal drugs were never part of my world and held no interest for me, I certainly gave the legal ones of alcohol and nicotine a bashing. Once while travelling in Hong Kong, I bought a charm because it looked pretty. I couldn't read the Chinese script that went with it and asked what it meant. Long life, I was told. How ironic. At that point, it was the last thing I craved.

Remembering to eat good, healthy food and not too much of it became a three-times-a-day discipline in caring for myself. I learned to pick my way through the menus of the fancy restaurants I visited, choosing the salads, lean meat and grilled fish. I took every non-essential restaurant lunch out of my diary and went to the gym instead. I started wearing trainers to work, like a New Yorker, so that I could walk to and from the office and to business appointments when it would have been quicker to jump on a tube or in a cab. Even deciding to take the stairs rather than a lift was a mini reminder to myself that I was worth looking after.

∞

Survivor guilt is a funny thing. I don't think anyone who hasn't experienced it can really understand what it's like. To outsiders it is clearly absurd to punish yourself because someone you love has died. Making yourself suffer is never going to bring them back. It's an utterly illogical but nonetheless very powerful emotion. And I tortured myself with it for years, believing that since I'd failed to save John and Ellie I wasn't worthy to live myself. But throughout that year, 2002, as I learned to take care of myself again I finally began to believe that if I had a life I might as well live it.

With the return of my self respect came the faint possibility taking shape at the back of my mind that possibly, just possibly, I could meet someone and form a relationship again. But by now I was 46 and had been on my own for a decade. I had the idea that if I wasn't going to be alone forever I probably had to do something about it soon.

I wasn't quite sure what form this relationship might take. I had been so badly hurt in my two attempts at romantic attachment since John's death that the idea didn't really hold much appeal. Certainly I wasn't looking for a father figure for Hope. As far as I was concerned she already had a father – he was just no longer available to us. I wasn't sure that I could ever contemplate setting up home jointly with anyone again. And heaven forbid letting anyone move into my house. After the long, hard haul of working out a way of living that suited Hope and me, I'd now got our lives organised to my satisfaction and I didn't fancy some unknown man trampling all over our sensibilities.

I think I just wanted someone to take me to the theatre occasionally. And to catch my eye across the table at dinner parties. To be there on my birthday, maybe? Birthdays were always difficult, a time when I felt most alone. Hope was obviously too little to be able to get me a card or a present without adult help, let alone organise anything else. One year though, Christina was staying with me on my birthday and she brought me a cup of tea in bed. I still remember feeling quite overwhelmed by the luxury of being cared for – even in such a small way – rather than having to do everything for myself.

My mother had met a man a little over a year after my father died and it had seemed to me to be deeply unfair that she, so comparatively recently widowed, had a partner while I was still on my own. In fact, sometimes it seemed as if the whole world was comprised of couples and I was the only one who was single. I became obsessed with checking out how quickly famous widows had remarried. Jackie Kennedy had married Aristotle Onassis after four years, despite the opprobrium of the entire American nation. It hadn't worked out that well, admittedly, but I disregarded details like that.

Nor could I work out how I was to meet anyone. Actually, I was meeting new people all the time though my work but I didn't want to complicate my work life with anything as messy as romantic attraction. Following on from my success in signing up for WeightWatchers rather than going it alone, I decided – on roughly the same principles – to try a dating agency and began researching them on the Internet. The choice is huge. You can sign up with an Internet dating service for just a few pounds but my friend June, in whom I confided, cautioned against this. There are few checks or safeguards so you have to be very capable of looking out for your own interests and – frankly – she didn't think I was. In this she was right. I'd been out of the dating scene for so long that I didn't know the rules of engagement. Actually, I had never really been in the dating scene and I'd certainly never been on a blind date. It was all new territory to me.

So instead I chose an agency which offered a more hand-holding service, although they charged what seemed like an awful lot of money. But, as June pointed out, it was only about the same as I would spend on a holiday and hopefully the results would be at least as beneficial as two weeks on a beach.

I was so nervous that I cancelled the first appointment with the agency, only making it through the doors on the second attempt. This is apparently quite good going. The elegant, friendly woman who ran the agency told me she had clients who took three or four goes before turning up. She was well used to the apologetic phone calls about urgent business meetings. But despite her matter-of-fact air and her assurances that dating agencies were by far the safest way for busy high-profile people to get to know each other, I was fairly appalled to be there at all. I felt it reeked of desperation although I'd actually discovered by this time that quite a few couples I knew had met each other this way. If people say they met on a blind date, or were introduced by a mutual friend who thought they'd get on, then it's often code for a dating-agency liaison.

Not only did I despise myself for taking this route, I also thought, simultaneously, that I would be turned away. I was worried that at 46 I was too old and it's certainly true that some agencies refuse to take on women over 40. Most will also refuse to consider anyone who's overweight so it was lucky I'd discovered WeightWatchers first. Some only promise a certain number of introductions or kick you out after a year, so they don't end up with old recidivists on their books, but this agency offered open-ended membership which seemed to suggest they had quite a good success rate. And they were prepared to take me on.

I don't know what I expected. Maybe in my darkest fears some sort of meat market, trading in the lonely, the hopeless and the desperate. In good moments, I tried to regard it as rather Jane Austen-esque.

The men I met – eight of them in total – were all perfectly nice and they mostly conformed to a type. They'd spent their youth and middle years working 16-hour days building up businesses, only to wake up in their fifties and find their long-suffering wives had left them and they'd suddenly got time on their hands and no one to spend it with.

Once I'd got over my hideous nervousness about the whole 'blind date' thing, I rather enjoyed my dates. I met a man who raced Ferraris and another who liked buying houses all over London and the South of France, including one previously owned by the writer Katherine Mansfield – of whom he'd never heard. There was a barrister I was rather fond of, but I wasn't sure he wasn't still also fond of his wife as he lived in a flat in the marital home. In fact, there were several who, while they were technically separated or even divorced, struck me as still emotionally entwined. But I went to wonderful restaurants and private members' clubs and drank champagne and had fun.

Nothing ever came to anything and I felt I wasn't really the type of woman any of these men were looking for. Too thin, too dark, too Catholic, stroppy and left wing. I wrote in my diary:

All these men – it's so odd, like the way the spring clothes flood into the shops after the long drought of winter. Last night I had a date with A who is 58 and the chairman of a PLC or two. I was clearly not his type. Within the first 10 minutes he had described the *Financial Times* as a dangerously leftist publication. We struggled through a glass of wine each then I wanted another. He leant over, clasped my hand in his and said it would never work out because I 'would want a big house in Islington' and he 'couldn't breathe the air up there'.

I wasn't upset. I didn't care for him either. Too old and pompous. The next day I rang the agency and told them it hadn't worked out and they said not to worry, they would find me someone else – and they did. All the men were well-off, well-educated and well-preserved for their age. Regular gym attendance seemed to be a pre-requisite of membership. Rationally I knew they were most single women's (and many married women's) idea of heaven but none of them did anything for me. I don't know why. Maybe it was my reluctance to fall for someone I'd met through an agency, or more likely it was that these men were at a totally different lifestage from me. Wanting to semi-retire while I – and I could hardly believe this myself – was looking forward to getting back into the world at last. Whatever the reason, I never really worked it out. But I did enjoy trying.

And the funny thing was that no sooner had I got the hang of no-strings-dating than men started cropping up all over the place. Not just through the agency. Whereas before I would go to formal dinners and struggle to make conversation with the men on either side of me, now they would be vying with each other for my phone number. It was as if I was giving off some sort of pheromones that were irresistible to the opposite sex. 'It's raining men,' I wrote in my diary. And it was. I was taken to the opera, to the ballet, and on moonlit walks along the Thames Embankment. Most of the time I had to keep my mobile phone turned off because while I was out with one date, another prospect would be ringing up desperate to see me. It was as if the girl I used to be had made a late re-appearance. And about time, too.

This was fun – a word that hadn't appeared in my vocabulary for a very long time. I was enjoying myself. I felt as if the last piece of the puzzle had been put into place. No one could replace John; I wouldn't want them to. And Ellie's death had shattered my life like smashing a mirror into a thousand pieces. But I'd put the bits back together as well as I could. I'd never get back the golden life I had before it all went so badly wrong. But I had a lot, so very much more than most people – a job I adored, comfortable homes, a great social life and the love of my surviving child. Really, who could ask for more?

∞

It was during this process of reinvention that Ian Katz at *The Guardian* asked me to write about the long-term effects of bereavement. I found it a profoundly cathartic experience, representing as it did a manifesto of my feelings about death. It was published at the end of 2002 and reprinted in the *Mail on Sunday*'s *You* magazine early in 2003. The final paragraphs accurately describe the point I'd reached by then in the grieving process.

It sounds terribly cliched but I do now take much more pleasure in the small day to day joys of life. In some respects, I think I am actually happier than people who have never suffered anything and live in fear of what might happen rather than enjoy-ing the here and now.

Given the choice, of course, I would rather not have gone through any of this but I had no choice. I am assimilating it and it is becoming part of me. The girl I see in my old wedding photos who has no idea what lies ahead of her seems like a stranger to me. This is who I am now.

I have bad days as well as good days and on bad days I try to remind myself that in the whole history of humanity, and still in many parts of the developing world, my experiences would be typi-cal rather than exceptional. What I've been through – although dreadful – is really only part of what it is to be human.

When I outlined back in Chapter Three the different stages of grief, the one I had most trouble describing was Accep-tance. It's the stage of grief that is most open to misinterpretation. How can you ever accept what has happened? Won't it always be an abomination that your husband and your child have died so young? Yes, of course it will. But only when I had incorporated the reality of their deaths into every fibre of my being could I truly start to process my feelings. Everything that had gone before in the grieving process had been a fight against the awful knowledge that I would never see them again and a railing against the universe for making it so. Only when I accepted that what had happened couldn't be undone and nothing would ever be the same again could I start properly to live again.

Re-reading those lines now I can see that I had finally arrived at that place without even realising it. And I thought that, having got there, that would be the end of my story. But, to my utter amazement, it wasn't.

Chapter Ten

∞

A MAN WALKED UP THE
GARDEN PATH

When Hope changed from infant to junior school, her teacher called me in and told me she thought she must be dyslexic. She was seven years old, obviously bright, with a use of language and comprehension far beyond her years, but she couldn't read. I'd suspected for some time that this might be more than just a developmental glitch but was loath to face up to it. How could I? Words were the reason for my existence. Through my work they were what paid the mortgage and put food on the table. Our house was full of books, newspapers and magazines. I would read to her not only at bedtime but whenever I got the chance. My mother would devise spelling games to amuse her at the weekend. But although we were endlessly positive and upbeat, saying that all children learn in their own time, the truth was that nothing seemed to be getting through.

I was devastated for her. Not for her future career prospects: I had long since abandoned the indulgence of looking that far into the future. To have a child grow up at all seemed more than enough for me. It was more that I couldn't imagine how anyone would get through what life had to throw at them without the blessed relief of escaping into a book. I remembered the times when Ellie, lying so sick and frail in her hospital bed, had nonetheless in her imagination been able to sail with the Swallows and Amazons, dance on the stage at Sadler's Wells or gallop on a wild Arab horse. How would Hope survive without reading?

The school offered to fix us an appointment with an educational psychologist, who would be able to give her a statement of special educational needs, which would qualify her for extra tuition. But there was a waiting list of several months. I felt so guilty at having failed to spot the problem before that I felt I couldn't afford to wait even a week – let alone months – longer. So I found someone privately through contacts at Great Ormond Street. She interviewed me and then said she would give Hope three sessions on her own to determine the extent of the problem and whether she could be helped. Hope was extremely reluctant to attend without me. When I had asked child development experts at Great Ormond Street about getting counselling for Hope after Ellie's death they had advised me that, if we could get by without, it would be better. Now I could see why. Intrusive questioning by an unfamiliar adult can add to the trauma and is best avoided if at all possible. The trouble was, it was no longer avoidable. Hope had to learn to read.

The tests were thorough and concluded that Hope didn't have any of the recognised signs of dyslexia. Nor did she have hearing or sight difficulties. Rather she had blanked out the whole of the period of Ellie's illness and death, when she was four and five years old, to such an extent that she couldn't recall any of the work covered in school. Not only did she not grow physically in those years but she hadn't been able to grow mentally either. By the time she was seven she was able to focus again on her school work, but hampered by not even being able to remember how to spell 'cat' or 'dog'. Although curiously she could manage words like 'friendship' which had come later, after the trauma was over. This was how we knew it wasn't dyslexia. The real problem was that she was then learning words on a very wobbly foundation, and any attempts to go back to the basics summoned up so many scary memories of difficult times that she would become angry and rebellious. No wonder she couldn't read.

The therapist proposed starting on the long, slow process of re-teaching Hope all of her Reception and Year One work but allowing space and understanding for her to express the fears it aroused. It was hard, very hard indeed. Hope hated going. I hated taking her. It seemed to take forever. She cried and begged me not to make her. I made deals with her and bribed her through each term. If you stick it out until Christmas we'll go to Disneyland Paris . . . If you hang on until Easter you can have a little holiday with Granny . . . and so on. The whole process took two and a half long years. During this time school was hard, too, because she was still struggling with the work. The after-school therapy sessions were misery. The escape to our house in Burnham at weekends became as important for Hope as for me. And thank God for the pony, because riding seemed to be just about the only thing she could do without a struggle. Unusually for a child, she preferred schooling and dressage to gymkhana games or jumping. I would take her to dressage competitions where, aged only eight or nine, she would compete against adults, often beating them. My mother noted that the only letters that made any sense to her were the ones used to mark out a dressage arena.

Slowly, so slowly I thought I would go crazy, she broke through the reading barrier. It was an almost unbearable process. I had no recollection of ever having to learn to read myself, and her sister had seemed to pick it up as if by osmosis. I have a video of Ellie aged three, doing a treasure hunt I'd made up for her and gleefully reading out clues like: 'Look behind the shower curtain.' Hope's slow, painful picking out of words ruined any sense of the story to such an extent that I soon wondered how slow readers could ever have any incentive to plough on. And

I discovered that learning to read is very much about predicting what will come next. How a sentence might end. What the next word will be. If you live in a world where someone is fatally ill, you quickly stop wanting to predict anything at all so reading is often yet another casualty of bereavement.

But we got there in the end and, backed up by the school, who had been so brilliant all through Ellie's illness, Hope not only learned to read but with each passing academic year she progressed until she was finally operating at something like her true capacity, and her anxieties about school fell away, allowing her true self to shine through at last.

But by then she was 10 and it was time to think about which secondary school she should go to. I had never considered anything other than a state school for my children. When I was growing up there certainly wasn't the money to pay for private schooling. What's more, my mother and my sister-in-law were both teachers and we were all of the view that a good state school education was much more rounded than anything an independent school could provide.

St Gilda's school, where both Ellie and Hope had been, is a Catholic school but typically inner city with more than 30 first languages spoken, and around half the children on free school meals, but I was constantly in awe of the dedication and enthusiasm of the teaching staff, and had never considered that Hope's needs could have been better met elsewhere. But I wasn't dewy-eyed about all state schools. While I'd done very well out of my own education, my brothers had struggled at a local comp, out in Essex, which was troubled when they were there and, despite the best and continued efforts of my parents and others, was failing 25 years later when it was put into special measures. I knew that even the most dedicated parents – and mine were that – can come up against a brick wall with a school that has just too many problems and too few resources.

I wasn't so fussed about academic attainment but I did want Hope to go to a school small enough that if she started to fall behind again it would be quickly picked up. More than 1,000 children passed through the doors of our local secondary schools each day. I was conscious that, in adolescence, Hope could revisit elements of grief that she hadn't properly been able to work through as a child, and I knew how hard it was to support a child who was having difficulties and how much involvement was needed on the part of the staff. Nor was I sure that Hope was out of the woods academically and I was anxious that in a big school we'd struggle to get her back on track if she started to founder.

So I resolved to move house to be close to a school that more fitted our needs. I wasn't unhappy about this. I had in fact been trying to move since John's death. We had bought the house in a rush after we got back together and he had never especially liked it, wanting to move but unable to once he'd got ill. So I felt guilty that it was the place where he'd ended his days. An entry in my diary records that I had an estate agent from the local firm of Prickett & Ellis round to value the house just two months after he died. Luckily, common sense prevailed and I realised that moving house while pregnant, newly widowed and with a three-year-old daughter might not have been entirely sensible.

Of course, after Hope was born I was struggling with two children and barely had time to breathe, let alone move. But I would read the newspaper property pages, dreaming of locations I could move to when life got back on an even keel. It had looked like that might happen in 1997, but then Ellie had got sick, casting us back into the maelstrom. And so we carried on in an unloved, unappreciated house until 2003, by which time I had been there nearly 18 years of which at least 16 had been spent wanting to move. It isn't a bad house. It's in a nice quiet street, close to the station, and has five bedrooms, which meant that through all the vicissitudes of nannies and au pairs we weren't, at least, living on top of each other. Some people would love it, but it was too full of pain for me.

Now with Hope's school difficulties I had the perfect excuse to go through all the upheaval. Fired up with energy, I took a long, shrewd look at the house, with a buyer's eye. And was horrified by what I saw. It wasn't a house; it was a mausoleum. Pictures of John and Ellie covered every surface. Artwork Ellie had done in school was still Blu-Tacked to the kitchen cupboards. Even the books John had been reading when he died were still where he'd left them in their same place in the bookshelf. Oh my God, I was Miss Havisham! Hope and I had been virtually camping out on top of the layers of lives left behind rather than inhabiting the house fully.

Clearing stuff away was hard. The treasures that John and Ellie had loved were easy enough to deal with. I wrapped them in tissue paper and packed them away in big silver trunks I bought from an old-fashioned luggage shop in Crouch End. But what of the broken, the torn or the things that had no especial value but still linked me to them? I emptied out a box of old broken toys and found one of Ellie's ballet shoes in the bottom and sat there holding it, lost in the memory of taking her at three years old in a pink, frilled leotard to the ballet classes she so loved. And no more tidying was done that day. The following day, I psyched myself up to start again and out in the garden I tipped over a pot that concealed stubs of cigars that John must have surreptitiously smoked over a decade before. I had to throw them away – they couldn't be lovingly packed in a trunk – but I was conscious as I did so that it would probably be the last time I found something that had touched his lips.

Every room was full of pain and memories, but I worked

all through the Christmas break and finally I got it clear enough to hire a team of decorators to come in and paint the house white from top to bottom. Then I called the local firm of estate agents I'd had in before – Prickett & Ellis – and said I wanted to sell.

On 15 January 2003, I opened the door to a tall, very tall man. I was struck by his dark brown eyes and warm smile. He told me he'd come to value the house. As I showed him around I became very nervous again at the enormity of the undertaking, and chattered away telling him I found the whole idea of moving very stressful. 'Don't worry,' he said. 'I'm here to make everything better.' My heart did a little skip, which I ignored. His name was Mark Johansen. He measured up, took photos and then, a couple of days later, sent me the particulars to approve. In them he'd described the house as 'charming', which struck me as odd because I'd never seen it that way. But I started look-ing seriously at new areas we could move to and waited for prospective buyers to look around my newly exorcised home.

Except no one came. This was during the build-up to the second Iraq War when the housing market shuddered to an abrupt halt and big old, slightly shabby houses, however 'charming', just weren't selling. I gave him a key just in case there should be any mad rush of prospective buyers while I was out at work. There wasn't but it was useful anyway as Hope and the South African girl who looked after her were always getting themselves locked out and they would ring up and ask him to pop round to let them in.

Mark emailed me weekly with updates on the lack of activity in the housing market. And then, when that became too repetitive, he would add in bits about other stuff like the fishing trips he liked to go on – I found out he was a very keen fisherman – and even pictures of his catches. Looking over my shoulder at my computer screen one day,

June commented: 'He's flirting with you.' I told her no one flirted with anyone by sending them a picture of a fish.

I just thought of him as a friend. After my flurry of dating I'd calmed down and was taking things a lot more philosophically. I hadn't met the one man who would fulfil all my dreams. In fact I'd decided that there wasn't anyone out there. It was enough to have had one great love in my life. Greedy to ask for another. Instead I had men who were friends; one to go to the theatre with; one to go for walks with; one who made me laugh; one I'd talk to for hours on end. And the carapace I'd built around my heart gradually weakened and then cracked until I was able to open up and extend my circle of female friends, too, not replacing the old team who'd supported me so valiantly through the dark days, but adding to them. One was Ruth Harding whom I met as a result of Alastair's marathon run.

∞

Ali had taken up running in his forties after being nagged by his eldest Rory over his general 'old-dad' appearance, but he wasn't very good at it, so it was a bit of a joke among us. In fact, I used to tell him he ran like a girl. At well over six foot Alastair will never be able to get his weight down enough to be a very effective runner. Even at 14 stones he looks emaciated and that's still really too much weight to be pounding down through knees and ankles that are more than four decades old. So when he'd rung me before Christmas to say he was going to do the marathon, I was cycnical. He asked me how much I thought he'd raise. Ten thousand pounds, I hazarded. And who should he do it for? I had no hesitation in suggesting the Leukaemia Research Fund.

'You know that will mean you're dragged into the publicity,' he said.

'It's worth it if you raise ten grand,' I replied.

But I did find it hard. His sponsorship appeal was launched in the Palace of Westminster in the Lord Chancellor's rooms. Hope and Ali's daughter Grace ran off giggling to play in the bathrooms and the cupboards and goodness knows where, while Alastair spoke very movingly about John and Ellie. Rebekah Wade, editor of *The Sun*, and Piers Morgan, then editing *The Mirror*, sparred over who could bid the highest amount to sponsor him – each offering more than the original £10,000 I thought we'd raise. But I felt disconnected, as if I were looking down on myself, unable to speak and even embarrassed by the awfulness that was my life. Then someone whispered in my ear: 'You and I should stick together. We're the doubly-bereaved club.'

It was Ruth Harding, whose first husband, I later discovered, was the vice-chairman of Chelsea Football Club and had been killed in a helicopter crash in 1996. Ruth had remarried but her second husband had died tragically young from a rare form of cancer only a few months before she and I met. Bizarrely, it gave each of us strength to think that we weren't the only ones afflicted by such freakish bad luck. We became firm friends and would shriek with laughter together over the unlikelihood of either of us ever finding true love again. Ruth used to say that men avoided even standing next to her for fear of being struck by a thunderbolt.

In April I took Hope to watch Alastair run in the Flora London Marathon. We had no very great expectation of how well he would do but the sponsorship had continued to flood in and, to my utter astonishment, he'd got more than £300,000 riding on him. I wasn't even sure he would finish but Fiona and I were just hoping that he'd manage to stay upright because a photo of the Downing Street Communications Director on his knees with exhaustion would be reprinted by the newspapers over and over again, haunting him for the rest of his days.

Incredibly, he did the 26 miles in well under four hours and we all ran up to hug him as, soaked in sweat, blood drained from his face, he staggered across the finish line.

'I did it,' he panted, clutching me to his soaking chest. 'I did it for them . . . I did it for John and Ellie.'

∞

With the spring weather and as the uncertainty over Iraq resolved into war, the housing market picked up and Mark rang me to tell me that people were wanting to look around the house. I was scheduled to go away on a business trip to Barbados but that wasn't a problem: Mark had the keys. It wasn't a long trip but while I was away I had several tearful phone calls from Hope. She was refusing to go to school. She had a sore throat, she said, or a headache, or a knee ache. Normally, I would panic at the slightest hint of illness – I was perpetually on the lookout for signs of leukaemia – but since she'd turned 10, becoming older than Ellie was when she died, I'd calmed down a lot. And anyway, even thousands of miles away there was something about these symptoms that didn't quite ring true.

When I got back I talked to her and, with a sinking heart, realised that she was terrified the house would be sold from under her while she was at school so she wanted to stay at home to guard it. I tried to explain that it wasn't like that, that it took ages to sell houses and you had plenty of time to say goodbye. We batted it back and forth for weeks until I realised that arguing was only upsetting her more. She was adamant. She didn't want to move.

So the next time Mark called me to say he had people who wanted to view the house, I had no choice but to tell him it was no longer for sale. He sounded surprised, as well he might, but said that Hope's happiness must come first. I said goodbye and felt sad that I probably wouldn't have any more to do with him. I'd enjoyed our email friendship.

If I couldn't move then I would just have to make the best of where I was. I decided to remodel the house completely from top to bottom so at least it would feel like a new house once we'd walked through the door. And I gave in to the fact that I would just have to pay for Hope to go to the kind of school where she could continue the progress she'd made so far. I found one, very small with excellent pastoral care, and only minutes from my office so I could get to meetings with teachers easily, if necessary. But I was furious at being forced into such a position, with the unending hammer blows of bereavement that were now stopping me being free to live where I wanted, or have my child trot along to the school at the end of the road. Clearly, even after all this time, there was not one single aspect of our lives that wasn't going to be smashed up and spoiled by grief.

So I was cheered when a few weeks later I saw another email from Mark in my inbox. Apparently, he still had my keys, which I'd forgotten all about. We met for a drink and he gave me back the keys and also gave me a book on fishing, in the vain hope that I might understand a bit about it. I didn't read the book but I did post him a suitably 'fishy' card for his birthday the following week. He emailed me to thank me and we arranged to go out for dinner.

Hmm! Dinner. What was that about? I tried to be guarded but he was so easy and open to talk to. He knew all about my history as a result of my article in *The Guardian* but he seemed concerned for me, rather than overwhelmed by it. I told him that everyone I loved died and that I was afraid of feeling anything for anyone again. I don't know why I told him that. I'd never said it to anyone else – not even my therapist – but I felt myself sinking into his warmth and easy-going good nature. Self-preservation dragged me back. 'Are you single?' I asked. 'No,' he said. Not married but in a relationship. 'Well, I suggest you sort yourself out before coming after me,' I retorted briskly.

And as I strode away from him, the strap on my Jimmy Choo snapped, causing me to measure my length on the pavement. I could only pray he'd driven off without looking back.

I went on dates with other men – several of them – but they didn't seem as easy to talk to as Mark was. I started packing up the house ready for the builders, finally getting rid of the bed that John and I had shared and buying a new one.

∞

I managed to fit in a visit to Downing Street where Cherie was very cast down by the article in *Marie Claire*. Supposed to be A Day In The Life and believing she could veto pictures she didn't like, she'd allowed them to photograph her sitting on her bed having her make-up done by Carole Caplin. She felt utterly betrayed when they went ahead and published against her wishes. The ensuing feeding frenzy, in which everything from her friendship with Carole to her choice in night-time reading and bedcoverings was dragged through the pages of the national press, had been dubbed 'Lippygate'. Without defending *Marie Claire* I told her she'd been too trusting, clearly as a result of spending too much time when she was younger studying and doing good works, and not nearly enough time hanging out with bad girls like me . . . the kind who end up as journalists rather than QCs! She laughed and changed the subject, asking me – as she always did – about my love life. Cherie is a great romantic and longs for all her friends to be happily married. We discussed my various 'frogs' – as I had taken to calling them – including Mark, and we agreed I was to have nothing more to do with him while he was with someone else.

That year I'd booked a whole three weeks off work for mine and Hope's summer holiday. It was the longest break I'd had since maternity leave with Hope and I had no choice because the house was going to be gutted; and Gonda, our mother's help, was going back to South Africa for the summer. It felt like a momentous decision. Through all the bad times I'd kept the demons at bay by working through them. Now I felt able to allow myself to lighten up. Something must have changed within me. It had, and there was more change on the way.

While I was away Mark called to say he had ended his relationship. He loved me and wanted to be with me. We talked every day, running up huge mobile phone bills. I was thrilled but scared. Everyone I loved died. I wasn't risking that again. At the end of our holiday he volunteered to collect Hope and me from the airport. This agitated me so much that I filled six pages of my diary, wondering whether I should let him or whether I should just get a taxi as I'd become so used to doing during all my time alone. On the seventh page, I concluded:

Here's a thought. I could just give it a go. I could just 'act' like I'm allowed a life . . . Like I can love like I've never been hurt. Like I have needs, too. After all, I've tried it the other way.

And so he was there waiting for us when we landed in the middle of the night. Hope fell asleep in the car and when we arrived home he whispered to me: 'You take her in, I'll park and bring in the suitcases.' After eleven years as a single parent, hauling sleeping children in and out of cars, I'd given up thinking that there might be someone who would want to share the burden with me. Maybe he really was going to make things better, just like he'd promised back in January. I surrendered. And in the end after all the pain, all the hardship, all the loneliness, falling in love with

Mark was like falling off a log. I hadn't even had to leave my house to meet him. The man of my dreams had simply walked up the garden path and rung on the doorbell.

Our first proper outing together was to the premiere of the film *Calendar Girls*. I was so excited to be part of a couple again after so long, to have that someone 'whose eye I could catch across the room', that I completely overlooked this might not have been the wisest choice. *Calendar Girls* tells the by now famous story of the women from the Rylstone and District WI who posed for a nude calendar to raise money after one of the members' husbands died of non-Hodgkin's lymphoma, a type of leukaemia. I knew that, obviously, but somehow I thought it would be glossed over – a Hollywood, sanitised version. Despite friends warning me off certain films and TV programmes, nothing I'd seen on screen ever really touched me. No fictionalised account had ever come close to my own experiences. So I was unprepared for the impact of seeing John Alderton's totally convincing portrayal of a man dying of leukaemia and the fact that while the story is obviously glamorised, so much of it rings true right down to the bitter row between the widow, played by Julie Walters, and her otherwise utterly supportive best friend, played by Helen Mirren. I sobbed throughout the film. I sobbed when Alastair got up on stage and talked about John and Ellie and the Leukaemia Research Fund; and later at the after-party when I met and talked with Angela Baker on whom the story is based.

It should have been a disaster. With anyone else I expect it would have been. John cast such a long shadow that I had never quite been able to visualise how any other man could find a way to be with me that accommodated his memory without being overwhelmed by it. But Mark was kind and funny and held my arm protectively throughout. And chatted with Alastair, who had left his job at Downing Street just days earlier and was being mobbed by the press, who portrayed him as somewhere between Rasputin and Machiavelli. And when I was overwhelmed with emotion and tiredness and too much champagne, he took me home and told me again how much he loved me and how much he wanted to look after me and Hope.

And she had taken to him instantly. Through all the years I'd worried about what effect it would have on her if I brought someone else into the family when, in fact, she'd been longing to have a 'dad' like all the other kids. She didn't grieve for John as I did. She couldn't; she had never known him. I'd tried to keep his memory alive but, really, he was just a fantasy to her.

Mark, who'd been raised by a stepfather himself after his father walked out when he was one, was very careful not to come between us. And, apart from a three-week period when Hope threw an entirely understandable fit and said she wanted it to be 'just the two of us' again, she thoroughly enjoyed having this big cuddly bear around who could be conned into buying sweets for her and persuaded to drive her and her little friends to parties all over North London.

In November 2003, about two months after the *Calendar Girls* premiere, I had to spend a night away from home at a conference. On my return Mark called to take me out for dinner. Hope was dancing around the kitchen telling me not to wear my jeans but to put on a pretty dress and re-do my make-up. Spray on some perfume. Mark arrived and I got in the car and we headed off to the restaurant, but first he drove us up to Alexandra Palace to look at the view. I wasn't surprised. North London born and bred, he loved to go there and look at his 'manor' spread out below him. It was a cold night and raining, but he opened the car door and seemed to be getting out. I looked to see what he was doing but he was on the ground. Had he fallen? No, he was on one knee with a small jewellery box in his hand, proposing marriage.

When we got home, Hope was waiting up for us. Had I said yes? Of course I had. It turned out that, the night before, Mark had taken her out for dinner and asked her how she felt about us getting married. She named four conditions:

She wasn't going to call him Dad.
He couldn't boss her about in her own house.
When we went on holiday she was to have the window seat on the plane.
Oh, and could she have a skateboard for Christmas?

He acceded to all her terms and she gave us her blessing. She christened him SD2B, short for Step-Dad To Be, and a few months later sent him a home-made card for Father's Day. On it she wrote:

Dear Mark
    To me, I don't really know what a father is. I do know from seeing my friends' fathers they are people who love you but I don't know what it is like to have one. But now I am starting to know. You are not even my step dad yet but I still want to say Happy Father's Day because it occurred to me that you might never have had a Father's Day card. So here I am giving it to you.
    Love your Step Daughter (to be)

Our friends, too, were thrilled for us, although Christina wryly noted that he was going to have to be very accommodating as I'd been on my own for more than a decade. Alastair seemed a little cool though. Understandable in a way since John had been his best friend, but – it just didn't seem like him to be jealous. Then I got a letter inviting me to a fundraiser he was doing for his next sporting attempt – this time the London Triathlon.

It was a pro forma letter sent out to everyone who might support the work of the Leukaemia Research Fund, and started with some moving paragraphs about John and Ellie. At the bottom he'd scribbled – if you don't like me doing this, just tell me and I'll stop! Suddenly, I got the point. He was worried that his constantly banging on about John and Ellie would damage my relationship with Mark, but he was torn because he felt he should to keep raising as much money as possible. Idiot!

I rang him and he answered the phone in his usual monosyllable – 'Yeah!'

'Don't do that,' I snapped. 'I might have been someone from the tabloids and then they'd write a story saying you're depressed . . .' He laughed and I told him he was being daft about Mark's sensitivities. I told him that I wouldn't even consider marrying Mark if he didn't respect John's memory – and as the words left my mouth, I knew it was the truth and was filled with admiration for Mark's big heart and selflessness.

The tension between Alastair and myself evaporated instantly but I couldn't help wondering how many other misunderstandings like that over the years had contributed to the terrifying fights and severed relationships.

∞

A week later I was struck down with 'flu. Real 'flu that sends you to bed, weak, achy and shivery with a temperature of 104 degrees. I hadn't been properly ill in all the time I'd been alone and I was horrified at the weakness in my body now that I had someone to look after me. Mark brought me paracetamol and herb tea and tried to make me eat, but I was a miserable, bad-tempered patient and I hated being dependent on him. After a week I could stand it no more and went back to work even though I was still feverish. I'd been out of the office a lot before I got ill on business trips and at conferences, and I was long-ing to get back to the security that was my office and my workaday life. At about 5pm on my first day back I got a call to say that I was wanted in the managing director's office. I made my way up there hoping it wouldn't take long as I felt definitely wobbly. But when I got there he was obviously agitated and showed me a typewritten letter he'd received. It was misspelled and ungrammatical, and it began:

'You may think she's all sweetness and light but behind the façade it's a different story . . .'

What followed was a vicious tirade — and naturally it was unsigned. I felt as if I'd been hit and literally gasped for breath, and then I cried. It didn't matter that it was a mad tangle of lies and misinterpretations. That on the occa-sions I was supposed to have been so mean and behaved so badly I wasn't even in the office, or even the country. I was stunned, and in my confusion wondered crazily if I'd actually somehow come back from my trips, rushed into the office and done those things I was accused of.

We discussed it for a bit but neither of us could work out who would send such a letter. The poor spelling and grammar confused me — surely anyone who worked in magazines would be able to spell? I never found out who sent the letter. When I was properly over the 'flu and my temperature went down, I made a conscious decision not to pursue it any further. I'd survived worse, far worse, and whoever wrote it was clearly hurting more than I was. They had to be if my tiny piece of good news could prompt such a vicious response.

Some time later I was lucky enough to meet Jane Tomlin-son, an incredible women who, despite suffering from terminal cancer, was running marathons to raise money for charity. She said that along with the incredible support she's received, she'd also had poison pen letters, even death threats — which she pointed out with a laugh was a bit ironic for someone in her situation. There are some really weird people out there.

∞

Mark and I decided to get married in the summer of 2004, at St Bride's in Fleet Street where John's memorial service had been held, and where George – who'd talked me out of wanting to kill myself – was now, incredibly, based as an ordinand, training to become a priest. For those like me who'd got to know him in his El Vino's days, George's vocation was proof that God really does move in mysterious ways.

St Bride's is known as the journalists' church which made it very special for me, but as it's Church of England, not Catholic, we had to get special permission for Fr Anthony to take part in the ceremony too.

We planned a grand wedding with a reception for more than 300 guests. Having organised two huge funerals I was damned if the blessing on the start of our new life together was going to be any smaller. And, in any case, I wanted to invite everyone who had been there for me over the years, in whatever way.

My brothers Jeremy and Hugh were giving me away. Mark's brother Paul was best man. Hope and her cousin Eva were bridesmaids and my nephew Archie and Mark's nephew Harry were pages. We booked a string quartet and – my personal favourite – a fountain of molten chocolate for the reception.

Unable to find any wedding dresses that would suit a 47-year-old bride and unwilling to repeat the knickerbockers experience of my previous wedding, I flew to Dublin with Christina who was my Matron of Honour, and we had suits made in silk crêpe by the lovely Irish designers Tyrell and Brennan. Mine, full-length in ivory, Christina's, knee-length in sapphire blue.

I didn't know what to do with my hair until Ruth Harding called me up and took me to lunch, then on to the jeweller's shop run by her new man Nigel – she had finally found someone who wasn't afraid to stand next to her. He lent me an antique diamond tiara and dangly diamond earrings that cost more than the honeymoon.

∞

It was all going perfectly to plan except for the fact that I was suffering the most appalling guilt.

'John wouldn't want you to live your life alone. He'd want you to be happy, to find someone else.' That's what everyone told me but how could I believe them? John was 35 when he died. A young man who should have been at the peak of his virility. Instead his body was ravaged by chemotherapy, covered in sores that wouldn't heal. The only salve for his battered dignity was that his hair had grown back between treatments. He knew deep down that he wouldn't survive; wouldn't live to see Ellie grow up or know his unborn child. He knew he'd never fulfil his dreams, or feel strong, or healthy or sexually powerful again. So how in God's name could he contemplate his pregnant wife finding happiness with someone else? When it comes down to it, why should the dying be any less jealous than the healthy? Indeed they have every reason to be more so.

In the run-up to the wedding my head felt like it was on the spin cycle in a washing machine as I fought with the reality that while the dying may be jealous, the dead are not. Mark was patient and kind as ever, often baffled by my rages and tears. Was I even doing the right thing? We had been together for less than a year. What if it was all a disaster? What if I was throwing away the independence I'd fought so long for?

∞

The day itself was beautiful. Everyone drank too much champagne and cried at the speeches. Then Alastair played the bagpipes and all the children danced.

Only one of my friends was unable to be there. I'd known Kate Carr for more than 20 years. We'd met on a work trip to Boston and stayed friends as we progressed through various jobs − she became editor of *The Sunday Times Magazine* − and had our families. In 1997, while Ellie was in hospital, Kate had been diagnosed with breast cancer at the age of only 39.

She came in to visit us and made Ellie laugh by dramatically pulling off her furry hat to reveal her head as bald as an egg underneath. She appeared to make a full recovery and, after a spell running the cancer charity Gilda's Club, settled down to life as a freelance journalist so she could see more of her children. I signed her up as books editor for *Good Housekeeping*, thrilled not only to have such an experienced and gifted writer working for the magazine but also because it gave us a chance to see more of each other. She was my happy ending, my good luck charm. My proof that people could suffer awful forms of cancer and survive. But then at Easter 2004 she was taken into hospital with excruciating back pain. The cancer had returned.

I went to see her and found her thin and dreadfully ill − too weak to sit up. She told me the cancer was all over and that she was going to die. We talked of how her children would cope without her. And we cried together. When I left the hospital my head was pounding and I felt sweaty and panicky. Too distraught to go back to the office. Now at last I knew how those friends who'd supported me through John's and Ellie's illnesses felt every time they came to see us. How hard it is to walk back into the real world when you've visited death's waiting room.

The hospital were hopeful that Kate could come to my wedding – in a wheelchair – but on the day she was just too ill. I called her from the departure lounge just before we left for our honeymoon in Capri, and later wrote her a long letter, telling her how much of a friend she'd been to me and how I'd valued her advice, using her as my 'touchstone' throughout the years we'd known each other. How I would save up problems I had until I could see her and get her cool, clear-headed advice. I prefaced the letter by saying that it was the sort of letter of commiseration I might write to her husband Simon after her death, but I'd come round to the belief that if you were lucky enough to get the chance to say it to someone before you lost them, then you should do so.

I didn't know how she'd take it. I knew that the dying waver between denial of the inevitable and acceptance, and if she opened it on the wrong day, or at the wrong time, it could be very hurtful. But she wrote back telling me how much she'd valued my friendship, too. And was grateful for the opportunity to say so.

So I thought I was ready for her death. But when it came in September 2004, on the eve of the publication of her book about living with cancer called *It's Not Like That, Actually*, I found I wasn't ready at all. I thought we'd said our goodbyes but then I discovered that if you love someone, all the words in the world aren't enough to tell them so. When you can no longer be with them, the pain is always unendurable. You can't do your grieving in advance.

On the morning of Kate's funeral I rowed with Mark and said I didn't want him to come with me. He stayed away but when I got home he was waiting to take me in his arms.

'You've spent so long suffering all this pain on your own,' he said, 'and now you can't bear it when someone tries to hold you. But I'm going to hold you and keep holding you until you start to feel better. And then I'm going to hold you some more.'

I didn't like it at first. None of the devices I'd used for coping with grief on my own worked when there was someone else around. Seeing my pain reflected in his eyes made it harder to bear, not easier. I've read somewhere that if you are suffering from hypothermia then even gentle drops of warm water can feel like fire on your skin. And that's how it felt when he tried to comfort me. But he held on and, gradually, day by day, I get more used to sharing the bad stuff as well as the good, the pain as well as the joy, to allowing him fully into my life and my heart.

And with that comes risk. The risk of losing him, too.

∽

There is no escape from bereavement, except by dying first. The more you love, the more pain you store up for yourself because grief is the price you pay for love. For a long time the fear of suffering more loss made me unable to let anyone new into my life. But that's not really living, is it?

Nor is it the best way to honour John and Ellie's memory. Because they wanted life more than anything. I finally realised the dead are talking to us, if we can bear to listen. And what they are saying is: Live . . . Live!

∽

One day, of course, Mark and I will be separated by death. Until then I choose love and life.

RESOURCES

Anthony Nolan Trust
To join the Register of potential bone marrow donors you must be aged 18 to 40, in good general health and weigh over eight stones (51kg). Men and people from ethnic minorities are especially needed.

The Royal Free Hospital, Hampstead, London NW3 3QG
Hotline: 0901 88 22 234
Website: www.anthonynolan.org.uk

CancerBACUP
A mine of information on everything to do with all forms of cancer. Use the website to find out what treatments consist of and to help decipher jargon.

3 Bath Place, Rivington Street, London EC2A 3JR
Tel: 020 7696 9003
Freephone UK Helpline: 0808 800 1234
Website: www.cancerbacup.org.uk

Cancer Counselling Trust
A small charity strongly supported by my friend Kate, which provides valuable counselling at subsidised rates for people living with cancer.

1 Noel Road, London N1 8HQ
Phone: 020 7704 1137
Website: www.cctrust.org.uk
Email: support@cctrust.org.uk

Cruse Bereavement Care
Renowned experts on all aspects of bereavement. Advice and information as well as support groups. Anyone who is bereaved should check out their website at the very least.

Cruse House, 126 Sheen Road, Richmond, Surrey TW9 1UR
Helpline: 0870 1671677
Young Person's Helpline Freephone: 0808 8081677
Website: www.crusebereavementcare.org.uk
Email: helpline@crusebereavementcare.org.uk

Home-Start

Any family in difficulties – for instance due to illness or bereavement – can ask for the support of a Home-Start volunteer, provided they have a child aged under five. Contact via your Health Visitor. To find out about becoming a volunteer contact:

Freephone National Information Line: 0800 68 63 68
Website: www.home-start.org.uk

Leukaemia Research Fund

This is the charity Alastair Campbell chose to support in memory of John and Ellie. Funds raised are used to support the most cutting edge research in Britain. They can also provide really up-to-date research and information for people affected by all types of leukaemia, myeloma and lymphomas.

43 Great Ormond Street, London WC1N 3JJ
Tel: 020 7405 0101
Website: www.lrf.org.uk
Email: info@lrf.org.uk

Macmillan Cancer Relief

Caring for people with cancer allowing them to stay in their own homes as long as possible. They looked after my father before he moved to the hospice.

Cancerline: 0808 8082020
Website: www.macmillan.org.uk

The Samaritans

Literally a lifeline for anyone feeling even remotely suicidal.

24 hour helpline: 08457 909090
Website: www.samaritans.org.uk

Sargent Cancer Care for Children
Provides social workers in hospitals, financial support and respite holidays. Very useful for helping families access grants and other entitlements. Recently merged with Cancer & Leukaemia In Childhood (CLIC).

Website: www.sargent.org

WAY
WAY stands for widowed and young. A network of support groups set up in 1997 for men and women widowed up to the age of 50. These groups weren't available for me but I have heard excellent reports of them.

PO Box 6767, Brackley NN13 6YW
Phone: 0870 011 3450
Website: www.wayfoundation.org.uk
Email: info@wayfoundation.org.uk

WeightWatchers
A purely practical way to get rid of pounds piled on while grieving.

Website: www.weightwatchers.co.uk

Winston's Wish
A small charity set up to help children come to terms with bereavement. Very helpful in explaining death to the very young.

Clara Burgess Centre, Bayshill Road, Cheltenham GL50 3AW
Tel: 01242 515157
Family Line: 0845 2030405
Website: www.winstonswish.org.uk
Email:info@winstonswish.org.uk

INDEX